HOW TO ENERGIZE YOUR VOLUNTEER MINISTRY

Susan A. Waechter and Deborah L. Kocsis

Marlene Wilson, General Editor

Group's Volunteer Leadership Series™
Volume 2
Group's Church Volunteer Central™

Loveland, Colorado

Group's Volunteer Leadership Series™, Volume 2

How to Energize Your Volunteer Ministry

Visit our Web site: **www.grouppublishing.com**

Credits
Authors: Susan A Waechter and Deborah L. Kocsis
Editor: Mikal Keefer
General Editor: Marlene Wilson
Chief Creative Officer: Joani Schultz
Art Director: Nathan Hindman
Cover Designer: Jeff Storm
Production Manager: Peggy Naylor

Produced with the assistance of The Livingstone Corporation (www.LivingstoneCorp.com). Project staff includes Chris Hudson, Ashley Taylor, Mary Horner Collins, Joel Bartlett, Cheryl Dunlop, Mary Larsen, and Rosalie Krusemark.

Library of Congress Cataloging-in-Publication Data

Waechter, Susan A.
How to energize your volunteer ministry / by Susan A. Waechter and
        Deborah L. Kocsis ; Marlene Wilson, general editor.—1st American
        hardbound ed.
        p. cm. — (Group's volunteer leadership series ; v. 2)
        Includes bibliographical references.
        ISBN 0-7644-2746-6 (alk. paper)
        1. Voluntarism—Religious aspects—Christianity. 2. Christian
leadership. 3. Church work. I. Kocsis, Deborah L. II. Wilson, Marlene. III. Title. IV. Series.
BR115.V64W34 2003
253'.7—dc22   2003022119

10 9 8 7 6 5 4 3 2 1   12 11 10 09 08 07 06 05 04

Printed in the United States of America.

Contents

Contents

Introduction

How to build an energized volunteer ministry that thrives . . . even after you're gone.

You're determined to move ahead with your vision for a volunteer program that supports and empowers your church's ministries . . . good!

You want to involve church members in appropriate volunteer roles that make use of their unique abilities, skills, and passions . . . even better!

You've got a vision that's compelling. A desire to see change happen. A commitment to see that change through . . . outstanding!

So . . . *now* what?

The remainder of this Volunteer Leadership Series is packed with step-by-step help implementing the management process Marlene shared in volume 1. You'll get lots of practical assistance putting in place the practices that will ensure you create an effective volunteer ministry.

But before we dive into the details, let's pause, take a deep breath, and talk about how you can build a volunteer ministry that's *energized*—that's going to thrive long term.

An energized ministry is one that isn't dependent on you to survive.

You may be the visionary who launches the ministry, or who helps it move to the next level, but in time it won't need you to survive. It's a bit like raising a child—in time you want that child to be self-sufficient. Energized, thriving programs are the same way. You're a steward of the program, not the owner; it belongs to God.

An energized ministry is one that finds its own pace and place.

By that we mean your volunteer ministry will probably change as time goes on. That's okay, because it's adapting to meet the needs of the church as *it* changes.

Twenty years ago, few churches had the need for someone to run the sound board or media desk; today volunteers have those roles. And in 1975 if you'd asked someone to handle the information technology needs of your church, you'd have been met with a blank stare. Now any 14-year-old nods sagely and asks what sort of computer equipment is in the church office.

For a ministry to thrive, it must have built into it the ability to adapt and change to meet not just the *current* needs of your church, but the church's *future* needs.

And to thrive, your volunteer ministry needs to have a place at the table when church leaders are determining budgets and priorities. Thriving ministries aren't afterthoughts or stepchildren; they're regarded as highly as other church programs.

An energized ministry is powerful.

Not powerful in the "I can rule the world" sense of the word, but in the kingdom sense of the word. Energized, thriving programs serve others. They praise God. They cooperate with God's purposes.

Energized ministries are also powerful because they're fueled by something. They roll on and on, adapting and changing as needed because somehow their tanks are being filled by enthusiasm, funding, and purpose.

Now is the time to make sure your ministry is adequately energized. A thriving volunteer ministry must be powered in four ways:

- It must be powered by people—including both church leaders and the congregation as a whole,

- It must be powered by vision,

- It must be powered by mission, and

- It must be powered by prayer.

In this volume we'll tell you how to design your ministry so you're energized and sustained by all four power sources.

Building a volunteer ministry is a great thing. Volunteers grow in their Christian faith, and through those volunteers other lives are touched. The mission of your church is supported. Your efforts in creating or improving your volunteer ministry will return fruit a hundredfold.

But when you build an *energized* volunteer ministry that thrives—one that keeps giving and growing long after your involvement with it ends—that's an effort that returns fruit a *thousand*fold.

If you're going to create, rejuvenate, or tweak your volunteer ministry, why not do it right? Why not create an energized, thriving ministry that's built to last?

You can do it—and we'll help. In this volume not only will you discover how to stay connected to energizing power, but we'll help you form a task force to help shoulder the leadership load. Then we'll show you how to transition from that task force to a volunteer director.

You'll also get a quick tutorial on how to ease your church through the changes that building an energized ministry creates. You'll learn to *gain permission* for making changes and keep your progress on track.

Energizing power. Solid leadership structure. Helping others embrace change. They're all essential ingredients in an energized, thriving volunteer ministry.

ONE
The People-Energized Volunteer Ministry

An energized volunteer ministry is powered by people—both the church leadership and church membership. Here's how to involve people you need in a task force that gets things done.

Some evening after everyone else has left the building, walk through the facility where your church meets. Perhaps you have your own building; maybe you rent or borrow a space. It doesn't matter—just go when the lights are dim and the rooms are quiet.

What do you see?

You see tables and chairs. Books and curriculum. Scuffed tiles and empty nursery cribs. Stuff. You see stuff. Lots of stuff.

But what you *don't* see is the church.

The "church"—the bride of Christ—is made up of people. *We're* the church, not the stuff we use to make programs happen. Nothing you see or touch or taste as you make your tour of the empty facility is designed to last for eternity (though the

> "People are the point, so invol- them!"

janitor might disagree about the dried gum shoved up under the tables). Only people are made to last forever.

And at church, without people nothing happens.

In your volunteer ministry, without people nothing happens.

People are the point, so involve them!

We'd like to suggest that you be intentional about involving several groups of people as you launch or revitalize your volunteer ministry.

The first group is church leaders. These are people who, quite simply, have influence. Others tend to follow these people whether or not the leaders have formal leadership positions. Their opinions are sought in decision-making and problem-solving.

The second group is the church membership. These are people who have a stake in your congregation and identify with the church and its ministries. As Marlene Wilson discussed in the first volume of this Volunteer Leadership Series, they have gifts to give and ministries to provide—but they may not know how or where. The vast majority of your volunteers will come from this group of people.

First, let's take a look at how involving church leaders can energize your volunteer ministry.

When Church Leaders Get Involved, the Program Is Energized

A leadership-powered volunteer ministry happens when most, if not all, of these identified leaders are making decisions that support the volunteer ministry.

What does it look like when the leaders in your church plug into your volunteer ministry and provide power and support? It looks like this . . .

- There's encouragement for the ministry—both privately in conversations, and publicly from the pulpit and in church-wide written communications.

- Resources flow to the ministry. Because the value of the ministry is understood and appreciated, needed resources (an office, supplies, time with the pastor) are available.

- There's personal involvement from leaders. When there's an appreciation banquet for volunteers, church leaders attend. When volunteers are asked to stand and be recognized in the church service, church leaders lead the applause. And when the ministry needs help, church leaders step up to personally respond.

Having church leaders actively involved is important because, by definition, where leaders go, others follow. Your church's leaders define the congregation's priorities not only by what they say, but by what they do. Where do they devote their time and attention? What church ministries get their undivided attention? What ministries get enthusiastic mentions on Sunday morning?

> **"Your church's leaders define the congregation's priorities**

If the volunteer ministry is among those favored ministries, the congregation will begin to think of it the same way.

As you develop volunteer ministry, keep in mind you need the full understanding and support of church leadership. You need it in part because the volunteer ministry is unique—it doesn't reside in just one ministry area of the church. It's not the exclusive property of the children's ministry or the administrative area. It intersects with all ministries within your church, because when there's a ministry there are usually volunteers. The person leading your volunteer ministry needs access to *all* ministry leaders within your church.

When there's a program or ministry in the church that isn't powered by leadership, there's often a poor outcome. Consider the following true story . . .

A Story without a Happy Ending

This story begins with a group of nine committed volunteers who wanted to bring a midweek children's program to their church. The program already existed in other churches, so the volunteers took vacation time from their jobs to go receive training in how to organize and run the program.

The volunteer team met almost weekly for months to get the program up and running, and one of the pastors was committed enough to travel with them to receive training.

It looked like all systems were go, and everything was running along like clockwork. The team recruited more than 35 volunteers to be part of the midweek ministry, from working in the kitchen to providing meals for the children and volunteers, to teaching a Bible study curriculum.

The first few months of the ministry went well. Both the leaders and children were having fun. Attendance stayed high and enthusiastic . . . until something changed.

The church leaders who had been so involved and excited about the program quit participating. The church staff had other programs to run, and before long the midweek program fell off their radar screen. Even the pastor who'd been trained to help run the program faded away.

Soon the volunteers noticed that paid staff wasn't participating, and the volunteers started to feel ignored. When the program's second semester was launched, enrollment of children dipped, and it became increasingly difficult to recruit and retain adult volunteers. Church leaders were actively soliciting volunteers for *other* programs, since the midweek effort was established.

Within the year a very painful decision was made to abandon the midweek program. The dedication of many volunteers was essentially negated, and to this day some of those volunteers have not become fully involved in other work of the church.

Was the decision to cancel the program a good one? a bad one? We don't know—but we *do* know one reason the program faltered was that key leaders pulled out, resulting in volunteers losing focus and energy.

The senior pastor can't be personally involved in every church program. That's not practical. But for church ministries to be connected and powered by leadership, *some* leader needs to be in the loop.

We also know of ministries where senior leadership participated for a time and then left—*but that was part of the plan.*

Everyone knew that the pastor wouldn't stay on the worship committee long-term; the pastor's role was understood to be temporary, so when he left it was with the blessings of everyone involved. He'd made his contribution during the vision and mission stages of the committee formation; now he was done. No one felt abandoned.

Had the team putting together the midweek program asked some hard questions (listed below), expectations would have been realistic and the level of commitment from leadership understood from the beginning.

And the program may well have survived the leadership crisis it experienced.

Without the support of church leaders, volunteers feel unsupported and unrecognized for their efforts and contribution. When leaders aren't actively demonstrating support, the congregation tends to have a lukewarm commitment to a church ministry. For better or worse, church members take their cues from church leaders.

> "For better or worse, church members take their cues from church leaders.

So you want the volunteer ministry to be energized by people in leadership. You *need* to have the volunteer ministry energized by people in leadership. How do you make that happen?

How to Create a Leadership-Energized Volunteer Ministry

There are two steps in gaining leadership energy for your program: Engage church leaders from the beginning, and keep leaders in the information loop at all times.

Engage leaders from the beginning.

Meet with church staff to determine their level of interest and commitment to a volunteer ministry. In the meeting, discuss the leaders' vision for the volunteer program and how they see the program impacting the church's mission. Share information freely, and allow time for dialogue. This meeting is a great time to determine who on the staff will serve as an "invested individual" and participate in the vision statement and mission statement meetings (more about those later in the next two chapters).

You can expect to hear that a volunteer ministry is important. Those words will be comforting, but what also counts is how church leaders will become involved and stay involved as the ministry develops. It's fair to ask some hard, probing questions:

- How do you think God intends for our church members to be engaged in service to one another and the community?

- How do you think our congregation will benefit from a more organized volunteer ministry? (Describe what a "more organized volunteer ministry" would look like.)

- What specific things can we improve when it comes to getting our members more involved in the work of the church?

- How would being more involved in a volunteer ministry benefit the members of our church?

- How much time will you commit to getting this effort started, and then to providing ongoing support?

- Where do you see the volunteer ministry residing in the organization? Who will be responsible for it?

- What resources will the church devote to the ministry (for example, financial support, people, space, equipment)?

As you discuss the leaders' commitment to the volunteer ministry, don't be hesitant to directly ask for support. Be

> "Don't be hesitant to directly ask for support."

prepared to define "support" so leaders know precisely what you're asking. Here are some possible questions that get at specific ways to provide support.

- Will you frequently refer to the volunteer ministry in meetings and from the pulpit?

- Will you describe the impact of the volunteer ministry on how our church is accomplishing the church's mission?

- Will you tell people you expect them to be involved in service through the volunteer ministry?

- Will you attend some or all of the meetings for the volunteer ministry? If not, what church leader will?

- Will you periodically write articles for the church newsletter about the volunteer ministry and what it's accomplishing?

These sort of actions set an example for the rest of the congregation and also cement your relationship with church leadership. They energize the ministry!

And here's some practical help: If you want to meet with your church leadership to present the volunteer ministry, consider adapting and using the leadership meeting outline on page 84.

Keep leadership in the information loop.

When we're thinking and praying about something, it naturally takes a place of priority in our lives. We identify with it.

That's one reason you want to keep church leaders in the information loop—so they'll have the volunteer ministry top of mind. They'll remember to pray for you and the ministry. They'll be inclined to send possible volunteers to you. They'll think of the ministry as a solution to challenges that arise in church programming.

But delivering information—reports, briefings, and statistics—isn't the only way to keep in touch with your church leaders. Consider these practical approaches for closing the distance between your leadership and the volunteer ministry:

- Create a recognizable logo for the volunteer ministry and use it often. It will remind leaders that you're out there and available.

- Create bookmarks for leaders to use in their daily devotional materials.

- Send simple, quick-read e-mails with messages about the volunteer ministry. Make the messages encouraging and upbeat.

- Create a button for people involved in the ministry to wear on their lapels.

- Insert a page of accomplishments or outcomes from the volunteer ministry in the church newsletter.

- Send birthday cards celebrating the milestones in the volunteer ministry to the leaders to share successes of the ministry. (for example: "Happy Birthday to our volunteer ministry! We're officially one year old!")

> "Be intentional about bringing the volunteer ministry to the attention of your church leaders."

- Highlight leaders in the church newsletter and talk about their connection to the volunteer ministry.

- Include a celebration during National Volunteer Week. (In the United States, it's usually in April.)

- Give a volunteer ministry statistic during each leadership meeting.

- Include key leaders on the initial task force (find out how to create a task force on page 19).

Be intentional about bringing the volunteer ministry to

the attention of your church leaders. You aren't bragging when you tell of the success volunteers are having in doing effective ministry. You aren't lacking humility if you draw attention to what God is doing in the volunteer ministry. Rather, you're celebrating a ministry that will bless both your volunteers and the church leaders who rely on those volunteers.

Consider this passage, where the Bible writer shares his joy at hearing how a friend is being faithful in his ministry and message . . .

> It gave me great joy to have some brothers come and tell about your faithfulness to the truth and how you continue to walk in the truth. I have no greater joy than to hear that my children are walking in the truth. (3 John 3:3-4)

Your pastor feels the same way. Brighten your pastor's day with a good report about what's happening in the volunteer ministry.

When Church Members Get Involved, the Program Is Energized

We like to think of creating a membership-energized volunteer ministry as creating a groundswell.

A groundswell is actually a wave in the ocean—a powerful wave in the open sea, the result of an earthquake, a storm, or another event far away. The wave can travel thousands of miles, and while they're sometimes hard to notice on the open sea, they hit the shore with surprising force.

Perhaps that's why the term "groundswell" has come to mean unexpected support that builds for a cause or political candidate. At first you may not even notice the momentum building, but then it's there, and it's powerful.

You want your volunteer ministry to have a "groundswell" feel to it. That is, it needs to have an exciting, excellent reputation that draws people to it. It needs to build power as it travels along. You want people to be *clamoring* to join as volunteers, and for the energy to grow as it radiates throughout the congregation.

A groundswell of support is spread over a large number of

people. It doesn't depend on one person climbing up on a soapbox and expounding the virtues of the volunteer ministry.

Groundswells can't be manufactured. They come about because something happens—an event, a success, a testimonial—that generates a response in people.

You can't *make* it happen . . . but you can *encourage* it.

And a great place to begin encouraging support is by creating a volunteer ministry task force that will in time energetically help spread the word about the ministry.

In the same way the senior pastor can't participate in every church ministry and planning meeting, neither can every church member get involved on your task force. In fact, you don't *want* every church member serving on the task force. The group would be too large and unwieldy. Nothing would ever be decided.

> **You're looking for people who will be the hands and hearts of the volunteer ministry."**

You're looking for a small group of people who'll infuse the ministry with the people-power that flows from the members of your congregation. You're looking for people who will be the hands and hearts of the volunteer ministry. You're looking for people who'll help you enjoy the benefits of synergy.

Synergy: 1 + 1 = 3

We often use the word "synergy" to describe what happens when people work together and a groundswell forms. Synergy is an equation that lets you add one plus one and get a total of three. Odd math, but it represents what happens when people join forces to work together on a task force or other project. Properly focused, their output is greater than the sum of the individuals working independently.

It's not a new concept. God describes synergy this way: "For where two or three come together in my name, there am I with them" (Matthew 18:20). One plus one equals three.

God calls us to pray and do his work, and he powers our efforts. That's the same power that in turn can support and sustain your volunteer program. It's what lets your volunteer program thrive.

Want to get people involved? Start by forming a task force.

Creating a Volunteer Ministry Task Force

A task force is a small team given responsibility for a short-term assignment with specific goals. The group isn't intended to stay together forever. It gathers around a specific task and then disbands when the task has been completed.

> "Want to get people involved? Start by forming a task force."

And that means you've got to be *very* clear about the specific task you're asking people to accomplish. What exactly do you want people to do?

We'd like to suggest that you form a task force around actually launching your volunteer ministry, not around just the fact-finding portion of the process. In many churches—especially churches of 500 members or fewer—it's most effective when the task force members actually take on key responsibilities such as creating job descriptions for volunteer positions and doing interviewing.

As far as recruiting task force members, you've talked with church leaders who may serve on your task force. You know people who are already volunteers serving in the church. These people are possible task force members. But you'll have to ask them.

You're asking for a commitment to work with you as you establish a volunteer ministry, or as you take your existing ministry through some significant changes. You want people to help you pray for God to work his will in and through the program. To help you design the steps necessary for achieving new outcomes for the program. To help you evaluate the progress along the way.

Your task force will get the new or revitalized volunteer

ministry up and running and then, when the time is right, transition into a different role—providing support and advice to the person selected to be the Director of the Volunteer Ministry.

Keep in mind that whoever is serving as the director does *not* want to be in the role as a "lone ranger." The director needs support and help! The task force will need to shift to a new focus, but there will always be a need for the involvement of good people who are committed to the ministry and its success.

> ## Selecting the right people for the task force is important."

Clearly, selecting the right people for the task force is important. In the next few pages we'll give you some advice about how to make sure you're pulling together the right team.

The following chart will help you think through a list of "invested individuals" who should be part of your task force. Your life will be easier if you keep the list short, but remember: If you expect your pastor to support the vision statement later, you'd best get your pastor on the task force early on.

There's simply no better way to energize your volunteer ministry with people-power than to carefully create a task force. Here are three things to keep in mind as you think about your task force.

1. Don't think you can make it without a task force.

It's tempting to just push on ahead without a task force, but you won't last long if you make that mistake.

The job of creating or changing the volunteer ministry, even in a small church, is just too big. Plus, when you involve people in the creation of a ministry they're more likely to go to great lengths to see it survive and thrive.

The people on your task force will protect and promote the volunteer ministry in your church and community. They'll make sure the ministry is supported, organized, improved, and sustained. They'll provide the prayer, commitment, and

"Invested Individuals"
Analysis Chart for Creating a Vision Statement

Who are "Invested Individuals" in the volunteer ministry? (could be individuals or groups)	What is their stake in the volunteer ministry? (e.g., they control the resources)	How can we get them to support and participate in the volunteer ministry?

(© 2004 Susan A. Waechter and Deborah L. Kocsis, Cornerstone Consulting Associates, LLC, PO Box 265, Midland, Michigan, 48640 (989) 631-3380.)

(Permission to copy this form from *Volume 2: Volunteer Leadership Series; How to Energize Your Volunteer Ministry*, granted for local church use. Copyright © 2004 Group Publishing, Inc., P.O. Box 481, Loveland, CO 80539. www.grouppublishing.com)

effort that makes your program thrive. They'll energize your ministry!

Remember: You're not in a sprint. You're in a marathon. You can't do it all alone or run the race without help.

2. Charter your task force.

Chartering is the process of becoming crystal clear as to what the task force exists to accomplish. It identifies the commitment needed and the outcomes

> **"Remember: You're not in a sprint. You're in a marathon."**

desired—what you intend to accomplish. Any group that intends to collectively work toward a desired outcome can benefit from the process, and an effective task force requires it.

The best charters emerge from discussions, and the following questions will lead your potential task force members to a thorough understanding of what's going to be required of the task force.

- Who is responsible for our task force's outcomes (for example, the elders, board, pastor)? How will we interact with that person?

- How will our task force be known in the church? What's our name?

- What's the mission of our task force? (Note: It will be different from the mission of the volunteer ministry.) What's our mission statement? Why do we exist?

- How will we know when we've succeeded and our work is complete? What's our vision for our preferred future? What outcomes do we desire to see?

- What authority does our task force have? What can we do on our own, and for what must we seek approval?

- Who on our task force will call meetings, communicate with the rest of the church, and perform other duties? What duties need to be accomplished?

- How long does our task force expect to exist?

- How will decisions be made on our task force (for example, by consensus, majority vote, or other)?

- How will we conduct our task force interactions? What are the ground rules for our meetings?

- To whom must our task force report about progress? How will we do that?

- How will we measure progress on our task force?

- How will we obtain feedback on our effort, and what will we do with that feedback?

- How will we celebrate our successes as a task force?

- With whom should we communicate and send meeting notes (absent task force members, church ministry area leaders, among others)?

Once you've talked through your shared understanding of the answers, ask each potential member to decide if he or she wants to sign on to work toward those goals.

Be clear you want people to make an *informed* decision about serving on the task force. If, at the end of the meeting, someone chooses not to join, bless him and bid him farewell.

Ask the remainder of the people to finish the charter process with you.

If you're thinking this might take some time, you're right. Plan on a two and one-half hour meeting. But it's time well spent, as this first task force meeting begins the work of creating the volunteer ministry or taking your existing ministry to the next level.

In the long run, it saves time to discuss these issues and to get agreements at the *front* end of your time together. If you wait until later, groups of people working together may become confused and experience conflict.

> "Get agreement at the *front* end of your time together."

We call this "going slow to go fast": going slow in the beginning of the process to go faster during implementation. Trust us: It's better to move slowly at the start so you don't speed along only to hit a wall later.

Sum up your answers to the discussion questions noted above. They'll become your charter. As soon as practically possible, put the summary in front of people and ask them to sign it—formalizing the process.

See page 87 for a sample completed charter document.

3. When the time comes, transition the task force.

Once the task force has completed its initial work, don't let the task force members wander off into the sunset. Instead, pause to celebrate! Throw a party! Make the transition a time of fun and joy as you thank people for a job well done.

Provide a time for refreshments and swapping stories, for task force members to affirm each other. And, if you've already identified the person who will be directing the volunteer ministry, let that person soak up the history of the task force.

> "Don't let task force members wander off into the sunset."

Be sure every member of the task force feels valued and appreciated. These are people who've energized your program—they deserve heartfelt thanks. They've provided leadership and accountability as your church started on the road to experiencing significant change.

And hold this thought in mind: The Director of the Volunteer Ministry needs an advisory committee or a board. The members of your task force are people you may want to ask to serve in that capacity. They've demonstrated they're committed to the success of the ministry, they're willing to work, and they've likely formed relationships with each other.

Energize your volunteer ministry by making room for people not just as "workers," but as leaders. Let your task force pull together those people God has gifted to help shape and reshape the ministry.

There's energizing power in a ministry built to thrive—and to thrive it must be more than just *your* ministry.

The Vision-Energized Volunteer Ministry

An energized volunteer ministry has a vision that inspires, defines the program, and attracts volunteers. Here's how to write a vision statement that makes your ministry magnetic.

The speech was delivered in front of 250,000 people on the Mall in Washington, D.C., on August 28, 1963. It may be the most influential speech ever delivered in America's capital.

Martin Luther King, Junior, stepped to a podium placed at the foot of the Lincoln Memorial, and in the cadence of a Baptist preacher launched into an address that will forever be known as the "I Have a Dream" speech.

Great oratory? Yes. Powerful imagery? Yes. But it was more. It was a *vision* held up for the world to see.

In 1963, there was no guarantee the American Civil Rights Movement would succeed. Some scholars and authors point out that the movement was essentially stalled when King walked to the podium in 1963. The March on Washington for Jobs and Freedom had proven successful, but what was the next step? Where was the movement to go?

Then King delivered his speech.

What King accomplished was to rise above the current challenges and paint a vision of the future—a future where equality was a given, where the benefits of freedom would be enjoyed by all regardless of color.

That vision energized the Civil Rights Movement.

Visions—expressed in passionate rhetoric or in simple vision statements—have enormous power to prompt action and commitment, and not just in 1963. And not just in social movements. A powerful vision can energize people in your church today.

The Vision Statement

If you want to benefit from the power of a vision, you've got to communicate that vision clearly and specifically. The way that's most often accomplished is with a vision statement.

A vision statement provides definition and direction for your volunteer ministry. It answers the question, "What would our future look like if we were completely successful in accomplishing what we want to do?" Your vision statement describes your preferred future—the way you'd shape the future if it were completely up to you and your task force.

> A powerful vision can energize people in your church today."

In Rev. King's case, the preferred future he wanted to attain was living in a society where color mattered less than character. The image he held up was one of America not as it was in August of 1963, but as it could become.

Your description of a preferred future needs to be just as clear and specific. Is it a church where every person participates in ministry? a church where everyone serves in an appropriate position? Is it a church where some of the members are serving in community efforts as well as within the church?

Your vision statement becomes a magnet that attracts people who want to help you achieve the vision you've articulated. It's your declaration of purpose and intent, the summary statement when people want to know what you're trying to accomplish.

For many people, the idea of crafting a vision statement is daunting. They fear it's difficult and complex, and that they'll be stuck for days moving around words on a page until every nuance is perfect.

We've helped dozens of organizations develop vision statements, and we can tell you from experience: The process is about as complicated as you decide to make it.

It's *important*—that's true.

It's *essential*—that's true, too.

It's *challenging*—no question about it.

But it doesn't have to be *complicated.*

We'll walk you though the process in the steps that follow. And please—*don't skip creating a vision statement.* It's the only way you can plug into the energizing power a vision statement provides and enjoy the benefits that come with it.

Here are some thoughts and suggestions about creating both a vision-powered program and a vision statement. This section will walk you through the process gradually. If you'd like a "cut to the chase" set of instructions, see the Steps for Creating a Mission Statement Worksheet on page 97.

1. Involve others in shaping the vision statement.

If you want to tap into the true power of a vision statement, get others involved from the very start. That's where your task force comes in.

When we do strategic planning with organizations, we talk about "gaining *shared* vision" in the organization. A shared vision is one that most people in the organization understand, talk about, and move toward together.

In a church with a shared vision, you'll hear people talking about that vision in meetings, planning sessions, and even the hallways. The vision is consistently communicated to everyone. And someone intentionally does things that keep that vision in front of church leadership.

> "Don't try to write a vision statement as a complete task force.

To create a shared vision for your volunteer ministry, include your task force in the process of brainstorming a vision statement.

But when the time comes to actually *write* the statement, don't try to do it as a complete task force. Instead, ask several people to draft a vision statement based on what they've heard the group say, and bring that first draft back to the task force. Then, as a group, you can revise it until you've reached agreement.

2. Do some dreaming.

The most powerful vision statements usually begin with dreaming. That is, you dream about your world as it *might* be rather than the world as it *is* or how it has been in the past.

You think about *your* preferred future—the way things would look in five years if your volunteer program accomplished everything God has in mind for it. What would that world look like? It's important that you and your task force zero in on some specifics, because the next step in the process is to actually describe that future you've imagined.

3. Describe your future.

You've dreamed about what your church and your program would look like if you were totally successful . . . now put that picture into words. Remember: Your vision statement answers the question, "What do we want to look like in five years?" You're not concerned at this point about why it's important to do it, or what the first ten steps of the journey are. Focus on where you want to be.

Maybe your current reality is that 20 percent of your church membership is active as volunteers, but 80 percent of the membership just sits. In your ideal future, 100 percent of the membership would be active as volunteers.

You might describe that preferred future in a statement like. . .

> The volunteer ministry helps First Christian Church involve every member in significant, appropriate ministry.

Notice that in just a few words the statement describes what the church will look like in five years . . .

- Every member of First Christian will be doing significant ministry.

- Church members will be using their abilities, skills, and passions for ministry.

For several more examples of volunteer ministries' mission statements, see page 95.

If this business of "visualizing a future" feels a bit mystical for you, don't misunderstand. Your visualizing the future won't necessarily make it happen. This isn't a New Age approach to creating a ministry!

Rather, you're faithfully describing what life would be like if God had already accomplished what he has in mind for your volunteer ministry. The power isn't in the mental image you conjure up. The power is in letting God infuse your thinking with *his* vision for what he wants to accomplish, then as a task force listening to God through prayer and stating that future clearly.

And, taking it a step further, it's agreeing as a task force that you want to *do* what God directs you to do in the volunteer ministry.

Remember that one source of power for your ministry is prayer. See chapter 4 to see how prayer must infuse every facet of your volunteer ministry if you truly want a thriving, energized ministry—and that includes creating a vision statement.

Do some informed dreaming, too. That is, make sure you thoroughly understand the current context of your church. Who's in it? Who are you reaching? What's your history? What are your current shared values?

Also, look at your environment. Is your community changing demographically? by income? by political party? What do those trends tell you about what it will take for you to be relevant in three or five years?

> "Do some informed dreaming, too."

Then consider how your volunteer ministry might look in five years. Who will you be serving in the church and community? What are the volunteer opportunities you'll offer? What paid and unpaid staff will you support?

With so many variables, it's unlikely that even with God's guidance you'll have an exact idea of what the future holds for your volunteer ministry. But as you dream alongside your task force members you'll sense a general direction, and you'll find that a vision for your shared future begins to form.

4. Be brief.

Notice that the sample vision statement on page 28 is brief. A vision statement is no place to use vague or flowery language; it's a place to be brief, compelling, and hopefully inspiring.

Keep your vision statement to no more than a paragraph, and if possible just one sentence. The most powerful vision statements . . .

- focus on a better future,

- encourage hopes and dreams,

- appeal to commonly shared values,

- state positive outcomes, and

- emphasize the strength of the volunteer ministry as a team.

When you've got your direction set and you've touched all those bases—all within a very short paragraph, of course—you're ready to communicate the statement to the world.

5. Communicate, communicate, communicate.

If you communicate the vision statement frequently, it can truly become the working premise for the volunteer ministry. You'll need time and persistence, and though you've communicated the vision statement so often you're tired of hearing it, communicate it again. And again.

There's power in repetition.

6. Build on the vision statement.

The shared vision becomes the basis for planning. Once you've clearly described the future, it's time to think about what actions are required to reach that desired future.

Having a shared vision is useful to your ministry—and to you—in so many ways.

- It provides you the opportunity to speak enthusiastically about what has happened within the volunteer ministry. Since the vision is endorsed by leadership (they're on your task force, remember), you won't be perceived as being overly enthusiastic.

- It clearly communicates to everyone what's expected, especially when volunteers are working independently.

- It brings clarity to planning and to implementing daily activities.

- It can be used in problem-solving and selecting opportunities for improvement.

- It prompts activity. We tend to move toward whatever we think most about. If we're thinking about the vision statement and the future it describes, we'll start to see more opportunities to act in ways that make it real. If many people are doing the same thing, we'll see synergy and teamwork develop naturally.

Think Outside the Box

There's a lot of wisdom in having a carefully worded vision statement that neatly summarizes how you see the future. But there are organizations that depict their ideal futures graphically, or through an art medium.

Either way works—so long as others can grasp and sign onto the vision. The precise form the vision statement takes is less important than the fact it's shared and regularly communicated.

If the smoking cessation support group has as its vision statement a photo of a broken cigarette and a crumpled carton of smokes, that's a shared vision for the future that everyone in the group understands. There's no need for words.

We think a written vision statement is something you'll eventually need even if you have a strong visual image. But if you can somehow enhance your vision statement with graphics, a logo, a piece of music, or otherwise—go for it.

About the only way your vision statement should never be presented is as words carved into granite. That's because your vision statement is subject to change; getting too attached to a certain wording or presentation of the vision is dangerous. God may update or change it at any time. As the future for which you prepare becomes reality, there's still another future out ahead of you—one in which you want to be effective and faithful.

> "Your vision statement is subject to change."

THREE
The Mission-Energized Volunteer Ministry

An energized volunteer ministry has a sense of mission that provides purpose and power. We'll walk you through creating a mission statement that keeps you on track and making progress.

It's amazing how many churches (and ministries within churches) aren't clear about their mission. There's no concise mission statement or, if there is, the volunteers and staff members have no clue what it is. They certainly can't recite it or explain it to others.

After creating a vision statement for your volunteer ministry, your task force's next step is to craft a mission statement—a statement that will help volunteers know why your volunteer ministry exists.

Your mission statement is like the foundation of a house. It's the solid base on which you'll build goals and objectives. It provides guidance about where to place volunteers and how to use your limited resources.

> "Your mission statement is like the foundation of a house."

A mission statement answers the question, "Why do we exist?" If a newspaper reporter stuck a microphone in your face and asked that question, your mission statement should serve as an answer. It defines who you are, what you're called to do, and who you're called to serve. If you know that, you're ready to answer the question, "Why do we exist?"

Some people in your church might view the volunteer ministry as a way to fill "helper" slots or as a method for getting more people involved. Your volunteer ministry can accomplish both those outcomes, but they're not at the heart of your mission.

You're wanting to implement the three theologies Marlene discussed in volume 1, and that means you'll do more than recruit "helpers." You'll connect church members with significant ministry opportunities that flow out of their individual, God-given abilities, skills, and passions.

The question is: Why do you do it?

Ready to guide your task force toward crafting a mission statement? Let's get started . . .

The Mission Statement

A mission statement is *not* the same as a vision statement, though the terms are often confused.

A *vision* statement describes your preferred future. It's about definition and direction—what you want to accomplish, and what success looks like. It's out on the horizon.

A *mission* statement is about why you're in business at all. It describes your purpose for doing what you do.

For example, your *vision* may be for your church to be a place where 100 percent of the membership is joyfully involved in volunteer ministry, with each person serving in an area of ability, skill, and passion. That's your preferred future. You'd know you're successful if you asked the question, "Who here is volunteering?" and every church member enthusiastically raised a hand.

But your volunteer ministry's *mission* is to connect church members with appropriate ministry opportunities.

Does your mission as described assure you that you'll reach the future you envision where every church member is volunteering? No.

Will accomplishing your mission move you that direction? You bet.

That's why you need a clear mission statement that nails your purpose clearly and concisely.

Why Bother with a Mission Statement?

What difference does a mission statement make for your volunteer ministry besides giving you something to print on your letterhead? Why should your task force go through the pain of creating a mission statement?

We'll share some of the benefits a mission statement brings to your ministry below, but let us highlight one outcome that would probably be a good enough reason all by itself: *Mission is a powerful motivating factor.*

Having a compelling mission, powerfully communicated, motivates potential and current volunteers when they realize they're a part of something bigger than themselves. Having a mission statement matters!

> "Having a missio statement matters!"

And before we move on, this caution: It's important you develop a mission statement *no matter how large or small your church.* Whether you're in a church of dozens or thousands, and whether your volunteer ministry is churchwide or designed to serve just one ministry area, it's worth creating a mission statement.

So . . . what will a mission statement do for you?

- **It provides information people need to feel comfortable.** Your mission statement answers the "why" question many people want answered before making a commitment. After all, nobody wants to sign up to do something insignificant or without purpose. Potential volunteers want to know that their volunteer hours will be well-spent.

- **It communicates philosophy and values.** When your ministry clearly states why it exists, it takes a position on what you believe. When you let people know you exist to place volunteers in significant ministry roles, you tell others what you think of volunteers (they can do important things) and what you think about ministry (it's accessible to volunteers, not just paid clergy).

- **It helps you set priorities.** Once you know your purpose you're able to develop a more complete understanding of what's important to do first, second, . . . or not at all.

- **It motivates existing volunteers.** In the long term, a clear mission statement keeps volunteers plugged in and plugging away. Volunteers are able to understand why their hard work matters and makes a difference.

- **It helps with conflict resolution.** An agreement on mission allows for effective conflict resolution. The likelihood of effectively resolving conflict is increased, because the focus is on fulfilling the mission, not on who's right or wrong.

- **It keeps people focused on the common good.** Your volunteer ministry exists to serve—to serve God, the church, your volunteers, and the people whose lives your volunteers touch. That's a lot of constituencies, and each may have a slightly different agenda. Your mission statement helps everyone focus past his or her own interests to the big picture.

> "You can't do everything or respond to every need in the congregation."

- **It helps your ministry stay focused.** You can't do everything or respond to every need in the congregation. If God has called you to do a volunteer ministry, do it with excellence. That requires focus. It's easy to drift away from your purpose when good ideas or available resources come along.

Having a mission statement served one group well in their decision-making process. A large Presbyterian women's group worked diligently during a retreat to create a shared mission statement. The shared statement they produced was:

> God empowers the women of [Church], united by the Holy Spirit, to serve Jesus Christ in our homes, church, community, and world. Celebrating our diversity, we model the compassion of Christ through support, nurture, and presence. Undergirded by prayer, we offer study, fellowship, and service to the glory of God.

Three months later, the Senior Pastor approached the group requesting they take on a new project he had in mind. The project was a great idea, and it would be useful to the church. The pastor decided the women's group might be the right group to adopt the project.

The members of the women's group spent about one minute reviewing their mission statement and quickly decided that the project wasn't in alignment with it. They politely informed the pastor of this. Although he was surprised, he was impressed with their focus. This story ended happily when another group within the church embraced the project because it fit that group's mission.

The reason to have a mission statement isn't so you can justify saying "no" to your pastor. Rather, it's so you can joyfully say yes to those things God has gifted and called you to do.

And—just like with a vision statement—your volunteer program's mission statement must fall under the umbrella of your *church's* mission statement. Your job isn't to strike off in totally new directions; it's to support the larger mission of your church.

How to Create a Mission Statement

Here's how to create a mission statement that energizes your task force, your church leadership, and your church membership. *And* that energizes your volunteer ministry!

1. Get the right people involved in creating the mission statement.

As with your vision statement, you want a shared understanding of the mission.

Plan for a meeting of invested individuals that includes time for discussion, debate, and—eventually, we promise—agreement. The process may feel long and tedious, but the dialogue is valuable. It reveals expectations and perceptions that will emerge eventually, so you might as well hear them early.

Use a process similar to the one you used to lead your task force through creating a vision statement. Decide who *must* be present at the meeting, who'd be nice to involve but isn't required, and who to not have attend.

Answering the three questions below will help you determine who's on your "must attend" list. Try to include people who can adequately represent others. You don't need every church leader involved, nor every member. Whenever possible have individuals represent groups of people.

> "We suggest that you narrow the number of participants at your meeting to fewer than ten."

• *Who are "invested individuals" when it comes to the mission of the volunteer ministry?* (This list could include individuals or groups, and it's likely you'll have some overlap with the people who were invested in the vision statement.)

One challenge you'll face when generating your list is that practically *everyone* in your church is an "invested" person! Church leadership cares about the volunteer ministry, and each church member is a possible participant. The list gets too long, too fast.

We suggest that you narrow the number of participants at your meeting to fewer than ten. It takes tremendous skills as a facilitator to keep a meeting with more participants than that on task.

If your task force is representative of the people you need, by all means just ask your task force to tackle the mission statement.

• *What is their investment in the volunteer ministry?* (for example, they hold the resources)

People can be invested for a variety of reasons and to different extents. You want to have several viewpoints represented as you create the mission statement. The following questions will help you determine the investment of the people or groups you've identified who have a stake in the mission statement:

How much does this individual or group know about the volunteer program?

To what extent is this individual or group impacted by the volunteer program?

What will the role of this person or group be in the volunteer program?

• *Should they be a part of the meeting to agree on a mission or just kept informed of its outcomes?*

You'll have to be politically sensitive and communicate carefully, but remember that not everyone in the church can possibly be included—nor does everyone *want* to be included.

Use these questions to help you determine the appropriate level of involvement for each of your invested individuals:

Why would this individual or group want to attend?

How will the participation of this individual or group help reach the desired outcome of our clarifying our purpose and focus?

Whose viewpoints are essential for effective, sound decision-making?

A practical note: You will never, *ever* find a time that all "invested individuals" can come together to discuss the mission. You'll have to strike a balance: The greater the participation in creating the mission statement, the higher the commitment and support your volunteer ministry will enjoy.

But if you wait until everyone can be in attendance, you may never have a discussion at all. That's why you've got "must have" and "nice, but not necessary" lists. When you can get all your "must haves" available, hold the meeting.

We've provided a sample meeting agenda and facilitator script on pages 98-106. Adapt it and other meeting scripts we provide as you wish; it's simply an example of something we've used with success in a variety of settings.

> "Don't rush through the crafting of something so critical as a vision or mission statement."

An assumption built into the material provided is that you'll create both the vision statement and mission statement at the same meeting. In a perfect world, that's possible—and desirable. But very often these become two different meetings, so don't feel discouraged if that's what happens to you.

Adapt the material as needed, but be sure you cover all the material somehow. It's essential that you don't rush through the crafting of something so critical as a vision or mission statement.

2. **Make sure your mission statement lines up with your vision statement.**

Your mission statement must provide the "Why?" to your vision statement's "What?". If you can't look at your mission statement and see how it connects with your vision, you're off the mark. You either need to revise your mission statement or rethink your vision.

Ask yourself and the people gathered around the table with you: "If we're really good at existing for this reason (your mission statement), will it help us create that future (the vision statement)?"

Don't settle for a mission statement that elicits anything short of an enthusiastic "yes!"

3. Be brief. And clear.

Long, complex sentences that leave everyone scratching their head have no place in a mission statement. You want clarity, and one way to achieve that is to be brief. Ideally, your mission statement will accomplish each of the following:

- *Educate others about the reason for your volunteer ministry,*

- *Keep everyone focused on what the ministry exists to accomplish,*

- *Prioritize where you should and shouldn't invest time and energy, and*

- *Quickly explain why you can serve the church and volunteers.*

These benefits won't emerge unless you're very brief.

Your mission statement will have power to engage and motivate people in direct proportion to its brevity, clarity, and passion. Eloquence may be poetic, but it won't capture anyone's heart or command his or her attention. Force yourself to be brief.

> "These benefits won't emerge unless you're very brief."

Be especially careful of including language that everyone seems to understand, but which isn't clear without an explanation. Remember: It may be that in two years none of the people sitting at your meeting will still be involved in the volunteer ministry. If your mission statement requires someone to interpret it, the people who inherit the mission statement will be lost.

A mission statement that says "We help people do ministry" is so vague it might include organizing bake sales to send students to seminary or providing rides to kids who want to go to church camp. Everyone knows that what's *intended* is to provide a volunteer ministry—but that's not what you said.

"We'll help church members discover how and where to use their abilities, skills, and passions in volunteer ministry roles" is flexible, but clear. It's a mission statement that provides guidance.

Here are three examples of mission statements that do a good job of being brief and clear:

"In order that all may experience and appreciate their God-given gifts and grow in their faith, we will empower, equip, and mobilize God's followers to share his love in service for the greater community."

"The purpose of the volunteer ministries program is to both extend and deepen the life of this congregation, and to more fully put into action our belief in the priesthood of all believers. Our goal is to enable each person in the congregation to . . .

- Discover and use his or her unique gifts as a child of God and

- Grow as a caring person, sharing time and skills with other members, with this church, and with the community."

"The volunteer ministries program in this church will enrich the church's mission through voluntary service by providing more members with opportunities to serve as volunteers in the congregation and the community, and by improving and coordinating our systems of recruiting, training, supporting, and affirming our members and volunteers."

If you'd like to see more mission statements, see the list of sample mission statements on page 95.

4. Keep the mission—and mission statement—alive.

A mission statement hanging on the wall accomplishes nothing. Mission statements are *action-oriented* statements; if they're not being used to direct action they lose their reason for existing.

Here are three practical ways to keep your mission statement in front of people and working for you.

- If possible, print your mission statement on documents used in the church—brochures, newsletters, and bulletins. You'll let the church membership know there's a ministry that will help them find ways to volunteer in the church.

- Make sure the mission statement is regularly communicated to and through the church leaders and ministry areas you serve. Your mission statement will help people understand the larger purpose of your ministry and keep people from mistakenly assuming you're just a glorified recruiter.

> "A mission statement hanging on the wall accomplishes nothing

- Begin all volunteer ministry meetings by reading the mission aloud and spending five minutes discussing key words or sharing stories about how the ministry is fulfilling its mission.

For example, one church's mission statement says, "We extend the healing ministry of Christ to those in need, so that we may deepen our relationship with God, self, and others."

You might begin the discussion by asking which word has special meaning to people, given what they're currently experiencing as a volunteer. One person might answer, "The word 'healing' is significant for me because I'm visiting church members who are homebound." Another person might say, "The word 'deepen' is important to me because I'm reading Scripture more often than I've done before."

5. Keep the mission—and mission statement—relevant.

Once a year, formally revisit the mission statement with invested individuals. *Do this even if you don't think anything has changed.* Why? Because . . .

- *You'll discover things you didn't know.* Perhaps there's a new area of ministry being developed and nobody has thought to tell you. You'll get information to start creating appropriate volunteer roles to support that area before the last possible moment. You'll also have the opportunity to get feedback about how you and the volunteer ministry are doing.

- *You can tell new invested individuals your story.* In the context of the meeting you can summarize the dialogue that happened when your task force created the mission statement. This is your oral history and your chance to make everyone an "insider" who has a complete understanding of the volunteer ministry's journey.

It's helpful to refer to notes taken during the initial dialogue—and ask that notes be taken of the annual meetings, too. Don't rely on people's memories—including your own!

- *You'll help invested individuals feel ownership of the mission statement.* Even if it doesn't change, the opportunity is there for people in the room to suggest changes . . . and that means the final mission statement has their seal of approval. They've ratified it. It's theirs.

Most mission statements don't change often. Only when the people you're serving in the volunteer ministry or what you're providing through the ministry changes will you revise the mission statement. But checking every year guarantees you'll stay relevant . . . and there's no power in a mission statement that's out of touch with reality.

> **"Most mission statements don't change often."**

Remember: Mission statements help you shape goals and objectives that will move you closer to your preferred future. Once your mission statement is in place you're ready to work with your task force to develop goals and objectives.

Or, at least, *almost* ready . . .

But before you get busy writing goals and objectives, there's one more place for you to find power to sustain your volunteer ministry. It's in prayer—and it's the single most important energizing source of all.

The Prayer-Energized Volunteer Ministry

An energized volunteer ministry is powered by prayer, both personal and corporate. Here's how to plug your ministry into this power source.

Have you ever run out of gas? Been driving down the highway and suddenly the engine of your car started to skip and cough, and then you could hear nothing but the wind whistling past?

Running out of gas turns any cross-country drive into a hike to the closest gas station. Because no matter how powerful your car's engine, no matter how important you or your trip are, if you run out of fuel you're going nowhere. You're stopped cold.

There's no question about how important your volunteer ministry is—it has the ability to literally revolutionize your church. If over the course of the next few years the number of people in your church who volunteer doubled, imagine the impact. *That's* significant.

And there's no question about how important this trip you're making is. It's vital. You're establishing or improving a ministry that will help people enter into ministry and service. That's *amazingly* significant.

"You need praye

So don't risk running out of gas.

Even being energized by people, vision, and mission isn't enough to sustain you for the journey. You need something more.

You need prayer.

You've Got Something to Pray About

When Jesus called his disciples, he ushered them into a life of service and obedience. He expected them to follow where he led. They entered into lives of ministry.

Plus, they were expected to bring others along with them. Not only did *they* have to get on board with Jesus' vision; they were told to recruit additional volunteers, too.

The body of Christ—the church—is a service organization. Ministry is in the church's very DNA. For a Christian to be involved in service is the natural state of things—it's how we were created to live.

Consider this observation from Dennis Campbell . . .

> The call to ministry is a basic idea in the life of the church. The Greek word from the New Testament is diakonia. Its meaning is service. To be a member of the community of those who follow Jesus is to be part of a community committed to service.[1]

If your church is like most, it *needs* an energized, thriving volunteer ministry! The ministry helps engage church members in significant service, which means you'll help your church *be* the church. It's a high calling to prayerfully, intentionally connect people with volunteer opportunities.

So understand this: *You're in ministry.* Whether you're paid staff or unpaid staff, you're in ministry. Whether you place fifty volunteers this year or just one, *you're in ministry.*

And like any person in ministry, *you need prayer!* You've got things to pray about—both for yourself and your role in this ministry and for the volunteer ministry. To create and sustain a volunteer ministry in your church, you want God's guidance. You *need* God's guidance.

It's tempting to think of the volunteer ministry as secondary to *real* ministry. After all, you don't decide if the church will launch a new building campaign, call on the sick, or do counseling with discouraged people. But you may well be called on to create job descriptions for the volunteers who do those things and to interview those people. Those front-line ministry positions may never be filled without your active involvement.

That makes your volunteer ministry not just a behind-the-scenes administrative function. It's a front-line ministry.

So let us say it again: *You need the power of prayer.* You need God's guidance. You need the discernment that comes with prayer.

But you already pray, right? What Christian doesn't?

What we're suggesting isn't that you casually pray about the volunteer ministry, but that you intentionally create a ministry that's *energized and powered* by prayer.

You Can Design a Prayer-Energized Volunteer Ministry

A *prayer-energized* ministry is one where prayer comes first. It's not just something we do after we've gotten ourselves into a pickle! It *precedes* our actions and opens our hearts to hearing God tell us what ministry is needed and how we can fulfill that ministry.

Prayer helps ensure that our volunteer ministry comes out of God's agenda for our congregation and not our own agendas. Ministries based on our own agendas are dependent solely on our presence and commitment. As soon as we become discouraged, move away, or get stressed, the ministry falters. That's not the sort of ministry that will thrive.

Ground your volunteer ministry in prayer and you'll reap short- and long-term benefits. And since the work of your volunteer ministry is the work of the Lord, why not let God run it?

Here are some suggestions about how to design a prayer-energized ministry.

1. Begin by valuing prayer.

How important is prayer to you? to members of your team? to your church? We don't mean to be insulting by asking, but those are important questions. It's not necessarily true that every church places a high value on intercessory prayer—asking for God to enter into situations to make his will known and to affect outcomes and people.

"Here are some suggestions abou how to design a prayer-energize(ministry."

The issues that accompany launching or revitalizing a volunteer ministry can be a tremendous catalyst for prayer. A vital prayer life will be a lifeline for your faith through what's coming in the months ahead.

Recognize this: Not everyone in your church will feel the need to join you in prayer for the volunteer ministry. Probably not everyone in your church prays regularly. Some people pray infrequently at best.

We point out those obvious truths because for your ministry to be successfully energized by prayer it *doesn't* require that every person in your church pray and fast for the ministry. That would be great—but it's not essential. What *is* essential is that you and a group of people who are drawn to the ministry agree to pray for God's guidance and direction and that you listen to God's voice.

And don't be mistaken: This isn't just a matter of tradition or habit. Prayer is an energizing force that can create enormous changes in and through your team.

Consider what we read in the book of James . . .

> *Is any one of you in trouble? He should pray. Is anyone happy? Let him sing songs of praise. Is any one of you sick? He should call the elders of the church to pray over him and anoint him with oil in the name of the Lord. And the prayer offered in faith will make the sick person well; the Lord will raise him up. If he has sinned, he will be forgiven. Therefore confess your sins to each other and pray for each other so that you may be healed. The prayer of a righteous man is powerful and effective. (James 5:13-16)*

From the very beginning, when you're creating a vision for your volunteer ministry, there's a central place for prayer. There's nothing more important than making sure your vision reflects what God wants to do with your ministry, that you're in harmony with God's vision. That involves asking God what he wants to do with and through you, and it mandates listening for an answer.

> Prayer is the act by which the community of faith surrenders itself, puts aside all other concerns, and comes before God Himself.[2]

2. Be disciplined in praying for your volunteer ministry yourself.

You're a key person God is using to launch or improve your volunteer ministry, so be available to God. Schedule daily time for prayer the same way you'd schedule time for anything else that's important to accomplish.

Countless books and resources are designed to help you improve your prayer life and deepen your understanding of prayer's power. Explore using one or more of those resources, or simply do this: Every day, come before God and say, "Here I am, your person in my world. I'm available for your use today. What do you have to teach me? How do you want to use me?"

You'll be amazed at how God answers those prayers.

> *"For I know the plans I have for you," declares the Lord, "plans to prosper you and not to harm you, plans to give you hope and a future." (Jeremiah 29:11)*

3. Pray corporately.

Ask the leaders of ministry areas to pray for the volunteer ministry at each staff meeting, and contact whatever prayer chain or intercessory prayer ministry exists in your church. Not only will there be regular, disciplined prayer for the volunteer ministry, but volunteers who already work with you will know someone is praying for them.

And there's another benefit: You can be certain the direction you understand from God for your volunteer ministry is *collectively* discerned. We once heard Sam Leonard, from the Alban Institute, say it well:

> Hearing the will of God individually that is not tested in community can lead to madness . . . This is personalized theology— "the blood of Christ for me"—not for us. Volunteer work needs two "yes"es: called by God and called by the church.[3]

When you understand that it's God's will that you move the volunteer ministry a particular direction, you can test your discernment with others. Share with them what you've prayed and how you heard God speaking to you. Corporate prayer helps you know you're faithfully following God's lead.

Identify a team of people who will become prayer partners for the volunteer ministry. Seek out individuals with enthusiasm for the volunteer ministry, others with deep spiritual discipline, and still others who have some experience (successfully and unsuccessfully) in trying to organize volunteers in the church.

> "Identify a team of people who will become prayer partners for the volunteer ministry."

Create a discipline or process for the individual and corporate prayer effort. Choose specific times, places, and methods for keeping partners in prayer. Prayer partners can meet for prayer time or make a covenant to pray at a certain time of each day.

Recognize and affirm that people pray in different ways, and this is not only acceptable, but valuable. Suggest that people may want to regularly ask God to help them notice with new eyes the gifts and resources of the church and the needs of the local community and world. Some may want to keep a short journal of these new insights. If a particular phrase or section of Scripture stands out as relevant to God's call to the church, encourage them to make a note of the passage and their new understanding so they can share that later with others.

Let everyone involved in praying for the volunteer ministry know that the goal of this prayer process is to develop an openness to God's leading of the ministry, so it can function the way God intends.

You want to join the psalmist in declaring . . .

> *I am your servant; give me discernment that I may understand your statutes. (Psalm 119:125)*

Share the results of your individual prayer experiences with each other. This will provide the opportunity for the testing of discernment from prayer, and you'll achieve both yeses: called by God and by the church.

Keep people praying for the volunteer ministry by keeping information regarding the volunteer ministry in front of them. Send out daily or weekly messages about the program to focus prayers on pressing issues. Be creative in all the ways you can put those reminders in place: e-mail, cards or post-cards, and telephone calls all can work. Create bookmarks, lapel buttons, or stickers your church members might use. We've even seen colorful and creative refrigerator magnets used to keep the volunteer ministry in front of people.

4. Pray specifically.

It's helpful to give people something specific to pray about. Following are some topics you can share to prompt collective prayer. Ask prayer partners to pray for . . .

- God's vision for the work of volunteers in your congregation.

- Church leaders to accurately identify the needs in your church, community, and world that could be met by volunteers in your congregation.

- Your congregation's commitment to ministry and service.

- Your staff's ability to support the volunteer ministry.

- The wisdom of individuals who are helping build and lead the volunteer ministry.

- The guidance of the Holy Spirit in the volunteer ministry.

- A fair distribution of work among your church's membership so the 80/20 rule does *not* prevail (20 percent of the volunteers doing 80 percent of the work).

- Increasing support of the volunteer ministry by the congregation.

- An ongoing renewal of volunteers.

- New connections to form with marginal members who could benefit spiritually from serving as volunteers.

> *Again, I tell you that if two of you on earth agree about anything you ask for, it will be done for you by my Father in heaven. For where two or three come together in my name, there am I with them. (Matthew 18:19-20)*

> "Here are some practical ways to keep your ministry energized by prayer."

5. Keep praying.

An ongoing dialogue with God about your volunteer ministry invites God to continue providing energy, wisdom, and compassion. You'll need all three!

Here are some practical ways to keep your ministry energized by prayer . . .

- Ask existing small groups within your church to adopt you as an ongoing prayer concern. Keep them in the loop about issues for which you'd like prayer.

- In the church newsletter or bulletin share some meaningful outcomes of the ministry (for example, the growth a volunteer experienced in doing a new activity).

- Include the volunteer ministry as a prayer concern during worship services.

- Include prayer requests in your church newsletter. This will also serve as a way to inform the congregation of what is happening in the ministry. It may even end up serving as a recruitment tool.

- Begin all volunteer ministry meetings with prayer.

- Personally take time daily to pray about the volunteer program.

Prayer and action . . . can never be seen as contradictory or mutually exclusive. Prayer without action grows into powerless pietism, and action without prayer degenerates into questionable manipulation.[4]

It's important you stay in prayer and that you're confident you're hearing God about your church's volunteer ministry, especially if you're just beginning a ministry. This is actually hard to do, because it's a natural human tendency to jump in and begin working on tasks as soon as a critical level of enthusiasm is reached. There may be other people in your church who are urging you to move ahead.

But prayer *precedes* action. Pray often, individually and collectively sharing the insights God has provided to direct you in service. Then act, create, and continue to pray for your volunteer ministry. Have the patience to wait for God's guidance, and submit to God's will no matter how much you think you know, or how certain you are that your way is the best way.

Pray as if your volunteer ministry depended on it.

In many ways, it does.

1. Dennis Campbell, quoted by Reuben P. Job and Norman Shawchuck, *A Guide to Prayer for All God's People* (Nashville: Upper Room Books, 1990) p.33.

2. Charles Colson, *The Body: Being Light in the Darkness* (Dallas: Word Publishing, 1992), 136.

3. Sam Leonard, The Alban Institute, from a workshop given March 4-6, 2002.

4. Donald P. McNeill, Douglas A. Morrison, and Henri J. M. Nouwen, quoted by Reuben P. Job and Norman Shawchuck, *A Guide to Prayer for All God's People* (Nashville: Upper Room Books, 1990), p.112.

FIVE
The Goal- and Objective-Energized Volunteer Ministry

You're charged up and ready to move toward your vision. Here's how to take the next steps by creating goals and objectives.

You're energized—by people, vision, mission, and prayer—and now it's time to put some wheels under your mission statement.

That happens when your task force develops goals and objectives . . . and it's time to do that.

You might typically use different terminology, but let's look at one definition:

Goal—This is the end you're aiming for. It's where you want to go. Goals are short-term actions by which you'll accomplish your mission. Or you might simply ask yourself, "What are we *doing* about our mission this year?" A goal is a broad statement that defines the "why" of your ministry.

The first draft of goals are almost always vague and hard to measure. For example, your church might set a goal of "sharing faith in our neighborhood and community." Good intention, but how will you know when you've reached the goal? When everyone has been handed a brochure about the church? When everyone has made a faith commitment to Christ?

When goals get specific, they become useful. A goal that has been sharpened and honed is sometimes called an objective. We think of it as simply a *good* goal—but let's use the term "objective" as you work with your task force. When a goal meets all the criteria I describe below, announce it has been promoted to "objective"; your task force will have something to celebrate!

Here's how we'll define "objective": An objective is a goal that has become a definite, measurable target. An objective includes standards of performance and achievement both for your area of ministry and for the people involved.

> **When goals get specific, they become useful."**

For example, the church with the goal of sharing their faith in their community can make their vague goal an objective by asking and answering questions such as:

- How exactly will we share our faith?

- What outreach events will we hold that are geared toward our community?

- When will we hold these outreach events?

- How many such events will we hold this year?

- Exactly who do we want to reach—what neighborhood, what age range of individuals, what ethnic group?

If you've ever driven through tall mountains, you know about switchbacks—roads that turn back on themselves as they zigzag up the face of a mountain. Because the roads climb the mountain gradually, cars can make the trip.

The *goal* of a driver is simply to reach the top of the peak. The switchbacks are like *objectives*—short, manageable, measurable steps to help drivers reach their goal.

When it comes to volunteers, many churches forget the switchbacks and just try to drive right up the sheer mountainside. No wonder so many volunteers burn out quickly!

How to Turn a Goal into an Objective

I'd like to suggest five yardsticks against which you can measure goals and objectives. If a goal measures up in all five areas, it's an objective. Promote it, celebrate it, and use it. But if the goal comes up short in any of these five areas, run it through your task force again to shape it up.

And be brutal: Promote no goal before it's ready! If people are fuzzy when they're *talking* about a goal, wait until they try to *act* on it. That's when things break down in a *big* way!

Yardstick #1: Is the goal specific?

How many? By when? At what cost? How will you know when you're done? Those are all things you need to know before you can delegate a goal to someone.

Some people become concerned that if you're too specific about goals (or any other part of your planning), you're not trusting God to lead your ministry. I don't think that's the case. By all means, ask God if it's his will for you to add four volunteer Sunday school teachers by next July, or if it's his will that you recruit an additional twelve male voices into the choir before you start Christmas program rehearsals. If you sense that the answer is "yes," then move ahead with the goal you've prayed about.

On the other hand, if you're not clear about your goal, how can God respond clearly? If you're praying, "Lord, please help me know if you want us to make the nursery safer and more efficient," I can tell you right now the answer to that prayer is yes. God loves children. God cares about children. Of *course* he'll want you to do the best possible job in the nursery.

But if you meant, "Help me know if you want us to add Mary and Jack to our nursery staff," that's an entirely different question.

And being specific is helpful in more ways than simply guiding your prayer life. It also lets you know when you've completed what you set out to do.

If you only say, "We need more volunteers to staff the nursery," are you successful if you recruit just one? If you don't say "We need to recruit those volunteers by April 1 of next year," then do the people charged with accomplishing that task have forever to get it done? You'll quickly learn that while specific seems scary (remember, someone might hold you accountable), it's actually a key element to reaching your objectives.

Yardstick #2: Is the goal measurable?

If you're specific—stating how much and by when— you've got good measurements in place. A goal is measurable if it includes clear wording about budget, growth, time, and achievement—all the specifics that might impact the goal.

> "A goal is measurable if it includes clear wording about budget, growth, time, and achievement."

Don't be quick to slap those measurements onto goals, though. If you want to achieve a goal by June 1, have a good reason for selecting that date. If you want to define "success" as hitting 100 percent participation in the church work day, is it a reasonable goal? Before you formalize the numbers and dates associated with your goals, consider yardstick measurement 3 below.

Yardstick #3: Is the goal challenging but achievable?

Set realistic goals. You want to help people stretch, but not be stretched so far they snap. Being handed an unachievable goal can be demoralizing and defeating. If the numbers are too big or the time too short, your volunteers may feel like huge failures—*even when they've done great work.*

Although you want to challenge your volunteers, you also want to be realistic when determining what you'll accomplish. For example, maybe you've been involved in a fundraiser for a new church building. Your stated goal was to raise $1,500,000 in two years. At the end of two years you'd raised $1,350,000. Did you succeed or fail?

You didn't reach the goal, so maybe the correct answer is that you failed.

But do you want your team of fundraisers—people who managed to raise $1,350,000 in two years—to go home feeling like failures? If you'd set your goal at $1,300,000, they'd be celebrating enormous success and be ready to sign on for whatever committee work needed to be done next.

Be realistic about defining success when you put numbers to it. Be realistic—but achievable.

And here's where goals *really* become objectives . . .

Yardstick #4: Is the goal delegated to someone?

If nobody is responsible to accomplish the goal (or each piece of it), it's likely the goal won't be met.

It's not just that people won't jump in and help—for the most part, they will. Especially people who've already joined your task force. It's that nobody knows if they're allowed to act on the goal. Will they be stepping on others' toes? Will they discover there's something they didn't know—like that the entire goal had been cancelled last month? And do they have the authority to accomplish the goal? Nobody likes to jump in and do something, only to discover he's wasted his time, or she's wasted resources and actually sabotaged a project.

Goals must be connected to real people, who have real authority to act.

Yardstick #5: Does the goal help you fulfill your mission statement?

You may create a wonderful goal that measures up to all four of the previous yardsticks. The goal may generate energy and excitement among members of your task force. But if the goal doesn't help you fulfill your mission, it's distracting you from being who God has called you to be at this time and doing what God has called you to do at this time. You need to set aside the goal and work on goals that *do* help you fulfill your mission.

The Hard Work of Writing Goals and Objectives

Many ministry leaders don't like to write goals and objectives. They think, You can't measure what we do in ministry; we do good stuff and you can't put numbers on it.

That sort of thinking leaves goals in some sort of ephemeral world. As long as leaders don't measure what they do, they feel good about it because at least they're accomplishing something—even if they aren't sure how much.

Or they fear that the moment they go public with goals they'll be held accountable by the board or the pastor.

But if you're going to accomplish something, you need to be bold about goals and objectives. If you state, "We need more volunteers for our program," that's not really an objective, because it's not measurable or specific. Instead, it's more of a wish. And it's a statement that no one can really hold you accountable for. If you recruit just two more volunteers who happen to wander in, you'll reach your "objective" without doing much of anything.

> **"Be willing to be held accountable."**

Be willing to be held accountable. Think through:

- Who is going to recruit new volunteers?

- How many additional volunteers do we need?

- When do we need these volunteers in place?

- How will we use them when we get them?

Getting important things done requires that we be willing to step up and take responsibility—in part by setting goals and objectives.

Maybe you can't accomplish everything right now—or ever. That's why you need to concentrate on goals you can achieve within a set time period. During this process, you also decide what you're *not* going to do.

As you set goals for your ministry, you'll quickly realize that there may be too much for you to reasonably accomplish in the amount of time you have available, or with the staff you have on board. You have to pick and choose which goals will give you the best return on your investment of resources (for example, time, staff, energy, budget). You have to decide what goals to not address because you simply can't do them for now.

How Your Task Force Will Operate

Once you've established some goals and objectives, it's time to decide who's going to take responsibility for them. Unless you want to see all the heads in the room turn and look at you (not a good sign), lead a discussion about how your task force is going to operate. That is, will the members of the group do everything, do some things, or simply give sage advice?

Here are some options to consider:

1. *Your task force members could divide up the major tasks and ask other church members to help them.* Each individual would take responsibility for a different aspect of the work (such as designing job descriptions, identifying potential volunteers, and training). This makes the task force a working group rather than just a policy group. This is often a good option for smaller or newer congregations.

> "Pick and choose which goals will give you the be return on your investment."

2. *Your task force might decide it wants to determine program and policy decisions, but use existing church committees or ministries to implement the program.* For example, the church nominating committee might prepare volunteer job descriptions and the church board might write the mission statement. Instead of doing the work, the task force will see that it's done effectively. This isn't good news for the person who ends up having to do the actual work of the volunteer ministry.

3. *Your task force might decide to focus on the area of greatest need and do nothing else for six months or a year.* For example, if no job descriptions exist for volunteers, the task force may want to spend several months just designing job descriptions.

4. *Or, your task force might decide it needs to find a director for the volunteer ministry.* This person—whether volunteer or paid—is charged with staffing the program and will organize and administer the details of the ministry. The director is accountable to the task force but might report directly to the

Senior Pastor. The task force can then devote its time to guiding, advising, supporting, and promoting the volunteer program among members of the church.

Note: One of the first things the newly-designated Director of the Volunteer Ministry should do is to find and involve a group of volunteers who will provide active support and help—essentially to function as a task force. If you can recruit a task force that will function in a hands-on fashion it will make that step unnecessary.

Have you made a decision yet about how your task force will function? If not, make this your top priority, and be sure to create an objective that deals with it!

> Have you made a decision yet about how your task force will function?"

SIX
The Change-Energized Volunteer Ministry

You're about to create some major changes in your church—and that can energize everyone involved. Or not. Here's how to gain permission to move ahead so your ministry thrives.

Some people love change. They're energized by it, and they love the thrill of the unexpected.

Unfortunately, they're in the minority. Most people hate change—at least change initiated by someone else. Unless most people see the need for change, they'll tend to resist it.

If you're going to create a thriving volunteer ministry, you need to gain permission for the changes you'll cause. Launching or revitalizing a volunteer ministry may change the way volunteers do their current jobs. It will change lines of communication. It will change what's expected of people. It might even change the staff configuration.

The good news is that with some planning and forethought you can nudge people toward deciding the discomfort they feel is a "growing pain," not another kind of pain.

If you don't do enough planning . . . well, you may experience what I (Sue) experienced . . .

The World's Most Expensive Paperweights

I was the volunteer administrator in a hospital a number of years ago, and we had the opportunity to computerize the reception area so we could retrieve patient information from the hospital's computer system.

The volunteers assigned to the reception area were skeptical about using these machines when the old index card files they'd always used were still functional (and familiar!). In the volunteers' minds, nothing about the way they were doing their work was broken.

So I provided all the reasons we should install computers. It would be so much more state-of-the-art to have computers instead of card files. Information would be more accurate and timely. It would be easier to update information. It would look more professional. The benefits were obvious, at least to me.

"What had gone wrong?"

I spent weeks selling the idea to the volunteers. They all attended the computer training that I'd arranged for them, and together we awaited the day the computers were installed.

Once the boxes were unpacked I set up the computers and got them ready for the next day's volunteers. I could hardly wait. When I arrived at work the next morning I rushed down to the lobby, and there, to my amazement, were two volunteers with the card files at their fingertips—and two computers pushed to the side. My computers had become the world's most expensive paperweights.

What had gone wrong?

Getting computerized was the culmination of *my* dream, not theirs. I'd sold the idea based on benefits I perceived, but I hadn't identified any benefits *they'd* perceive. All they saw was the need to master a complicated system they hadn't requested, didn't want, and could live without.

Ouch.

I slowed down and started over, spending time helping them discover benefits from their perspective. I allowed them to gradually get more familiar and comfortable with the computers. Eventually, the volunteers came around and the computers earned a spot on our reception desk.

Was installing computers the right thing for the hospital, and did it meet the needs of the hospital clients? Absolutely. Had I effectively managed the change in the volunteers' eyes?

Absolutely not. I didn't consider the losses they would experience—no matter how positive and small the changes seemed to me.

Sometimes changes made in church strike people the same way my changes struck the hospital volunteers. The changes are thrust on people without sufficient time for ending the "way we've always done it" and integrating the new way. People naturally prefer what's familiar, and change represents the unknown.

And your speeches about the benefits from your perspective will fall on deaf ears. Until people discover for *themselves* that making the change is worthwhile, you won't gain permission to lead the charge into bringing about change.

We've observed over the years that congregations seldom respond warmly when someone messes with the "things of faith."

We remember an interim pastor who used a different rhythm when reciting the Lord's Prayer. It so annoyed some of the church members that they griped about it for weeks. The pastor had used the same words. The exact same content. But varying the rhythm was enough to set off a month-long conversation during coffee-hour.

How you go about gaining permission to lead change can make or break your volunteer ministry.

How to Gain Permission to Make Changes in Your Church

There are several ways you can help members in the church deal with change and reassure them that it's positive to embrace the change you're proposing.

Most approaches involve face-to-face conversations where you can establish that you're capable of leading the change, establish that you have no ulterior motives, and explain the change clearly. It's also important that you allow enough time for people to discover the good things that will come about as a result of the change and to let go of the past.

Consider these practical suggestions.

Help people articulate why things must change.

Del Poling, a consultant who helps churches deal with conflict and change, shared a truly wonderful question with us recently. When Del engages in discussions with a church about change he begins the process with these questions:

Who are we? And . . .

> "Why can't we stay where we are?"

Where are we now?

After the group discusses who they are, what their ministries include, and what their strengths and weaknesses are, he asks them to answer this third question—the wonderful one I mentioned earlier:

Why can't we stay where we are?

What a profound question! It's all well and good for us to describe what we want the future of our congregation to look like. We need to do that. But until we feel the pain of staying in our present situation, we won't be motivated to push ahead into that new, unfamiliar future. As people answer the question they take on the role of change-agents, suggesting why things should change. They begin to get energized about making a shift, rather than resenting it.

Del told us about a church that asked him to facilitate strategic planning with the church elders. Del knew the church building included a gorgeous parlor, an attractive sanctuary, a welcoming fellowship hall, and a deplorable, run-down Christian education area.

Del asked the person arranging the first meeting to hold it in the Christian education area. When the meeting was scheduled to begin it was raining, and the meeting attendees sat in an uncomfortable, cramped room where the windows were leaking and wind blew through.

Finally, one leader said, "We can't stay in here any longer!"

That moment presented a memorable opportunity for the group to realize they couldn't stay where they were in how they offered Christian education, either.

This experience was a compelling illustration of what needed to change in that church. Until the leaders experienced the pain of the present, they were not motivated to move into the future.

Some additional questions to ask in regards to your volunteer ministry are:

- What happens now when church members try to serve as volunteers?

- What pain happens in their experience?

- If we keep things exactly as they are, what will be the consequences?

- In what ways are we failing to live up to our commitment to be disciples of Christ?

- What do we need to leave behind if we want to become better disciples of Christ?

Facilitate a dialogue about the coming change.

Remember—for your volunteer ministry to thrive you've got to help others discover for themselves the benefits of making the changes you know are coming. Your lectures won't do the trick. You've got to get people engaged in dialogue.

Use the same techniques and skills you used to plug church leadership into your ministry. Start by determining who should be involved in the dialogue, who are the invested individuals. Include key decision-makers who have the power to be a barrier to the volunteer ministry either through direct action or by passively not supporting the ministry.

Also include anyone who's expressed an interest in the program, and anyone who's expected to carry out program functions. And most *definitely* include people who control resources the program needs such as money, office space, or equipment. They can starve you out if they don't support the volunteer ministry.

Another person to bring on board is the person who'll direct the ministry, if that person has been identified.

And be sure to include those folks we call the "Reed People." These people have the power or position to hinder your program. If you fail to include them in the dialogue, they'll hang in the reeds and wait for an opportunity to shoot you out of the water.

Get these people together for a discussion. Use the dialogue about change agenda on page 92 to help direct the meeting.

Help people manage the transitions of change.

In his book *Managing Transitions*, William Bridges describes the stages of change. He writes that it isn't changes that are difficult, it's transitions. "*Change* is not the same as transition. Change is situational: the new site, the new boss, the new team roles, the new policy. *Transition* is the psychological process people go through to come to terms with the new situation. Change is external, transition is internal."[1]

> And be sure to include those folks we call the 'Reed People.'"

How true! But the good news is that there are three steps you can help people go through that will enable them to transition through change.

Say goodbye to the old way.

In your case, it's the way your church has always recruited volunteers and how you've always worked together.

You can help people say goodbye by . . .

Identifying who's losing what. Talk with people to find out what will be hard to let go of. It might be power or a position. It may be that they worked for years with their best friends and now they won't be on the same volunteer teams. They might be required to work in a new place that's more in line with their abilities, skills, and passions. They might even be asked to give up their favorite job!

Validating those losses for individuals. Listen as people talk about the loss they're experiencing, and fully accept that it's painful no matter how small the loss may seem to you.

Allow people to grieve openly. Give people permission to talk openly about their sadness or even anger.

Continue to give people information. In the absence of information, people tend to assume the worst. The more information you can share about what's happening with the volunteer program, the better.

Make the goodbye final. If necessary, tell people the old way will no longer work. I had to finally remove the card files from the reception desk in the hospital so that they were no longer available to use.

Celebrate the past with respect. Talk about the way things were done with respect. Don't invalidate the past.

Transition toward the new way.

This is the period of time when new things are being introduced and people are still unsure of what's expected. They also wonder what things will look like when everything is in place.

Pray for people to not find the transition too confusing or uncomfortable. It's aggravating to have to deal with change on someone else's schedule, especially when you don't see the need. Ask God to guard the hearts of your volunteers from bitterness or disappointment. Even better—ask God to energize your volunteers for change!

> "Ask God to energize your volunteers for change!"

Acknowledge that it may be a difficult time. Some people will accept the new approach to volunteer ministry quicker than others. Some people may never accept it. Let people know you understand it may be hard to make the changes.

Redefine this period. The change being experienced isn't watching a ship go down. It's taking a last voyage on one ship and then boarding another—a ship heading toward an exciting destination.

Be clear about processes and procedures. Be specific about how you expect people to do things at this time, even if the processes are temporary.

Keep talking. Create a small team to help facilitate dialogue through the transition, expressing feelings and concerns back to leadership.

Begin the new way.

This is the exciting, energizing initiation of the new way of doing things and working together.

Pray for everyone to see God's vision for the volunteer program at your church, and pray that everyone remains faithful to that vision. The changes you're making aren't random or thoughtless; they're designed to help you more faithfully fulfill God's vision for your program. They're important.

Communicate the big picture and why the volunteer ministry is changing. Do this through newsletters, in meetings, and from the pulpit. Don't rely on one communication channel to reach everyone.

Paint the picture of how it will be when the change is completely integrated into day-to-day life. You can begin to create familiarity with the vision of how things could be.

Ask people what they need during this time. Especially if you see them struggling with new ways of doing things, ask people what information or resources they lack. Be gentle and kind.

Celebrate and give praise to God for the success of the change.

And here's one last practical idea for encouraging the change process. In a staff meeting or other appropriate gathering, ask people to decide for themselves whether they're just beginning to deal with the change or have already moved through the transition completely.

Ask people to stand somewhere along an imaginary line in the room, with "just beginning to accept and deal with the change" at one wall, and "fully accept the change" at the other wall. Tell people to stand at one extreme or the other, or anywhere in between—whatever spot represents where they are emotionally.

This technique provides an opportunity for people to discuss what barriers or struggles they're experiencing. It also allows people who are further along with the change to provide encouragement to those who are struggling.

1. William Bridges, *Managing Transitions—Making the Most of Change* (Reading, Mass.: Addison-Wesley Publishing, 1991), p.3.

SEVEN

The Leadership-Energized Volunteer Ministry

A task force can take you just so far. It's time to put someone in charge . . . someone who'll keep the volunteer ministry energized and on task.

It's great to have a task force create a vision statement, mission statement, goals, and objectives. Having representatives from each of the volunteer ministry's constituent groups guarantees that you'll design documents that have widespread support and wisdom.

But you *don't* want to have a committee making day-to-day decisions as you implement those goals and objectives. That's a cumbersome process that will slow down decision-making dramatically.

It's not that you never want to reconvene your task force. You may well need one often as the ministry develops and grows. And many of these people may serve as an ongoing board of advisors, if you structure your ministry to include a board. (Hint: Reasons that's wise will be discussed later!)

But for daily decisions? It's important you find a Volunteer Manager to run the show.

> "It's important yo find a Volunteer Manager to run the show."

What Do You Call Your Leader?

There are several common titles in use for the person who directs and manages the volunteer recruitment and placement process in a church. *Volunteer Manager* is one common title, as is *Director of Volunteers*. Some churches communicate the importance of the role by referring to this person as the *Pastor of Congregational Involvement* or another title that prominently includes "pastor."

Pick whatever title works for your church and communicates the role clearly, but be aware that first impressions count. There's some wisdom in using the term "Pastor" or "Minister" in the title if you want to notify the church that the volunteer ministry is worthy of respect and attention.

However, for ease, we'll refer to the role as Volunteer Manager for the duration of this volume.

Take Me to Your Leader

The Volunteer Manager may be paid staff or unpaid staff. It may be a full-time or part-time position. In some cases, the position is staffed by several people who have a "job-share" situation.

But however the role is staffed, the basic responsibilities of the Volunteer Manager remain the same: to identify the ministries that can benefit from volunteer involvement, to recruit volunteers, to promote the volunteer ministry, to interview volunteers, to screen volunteers, to place volunteers in positions, to orient and train volunteers, to ensure supervision for volunteers (defining who volunteers are accountable to), and to evaluate and ensure recognition of volunteers.

That's a *lot* to get accomplished! Small wonder the Volunteer Manager needs a group of people who'll help!

When you're putting a Volunteer Manager in place, you need a job description that captures the essential information. *Even if you're the Volunteer Manager yourself, you need a job description!* It's one way your Volunteer Manager can stay focused, do what's most important, and be evaluated.

Here's a template for creating a job description for this role:

Title: Volunteer Manager

Position Summary: a paragraph describing the duties and responsibilities of the position

The Strategic Fit: how the volunteer ministry fits into and supports the overall strategy of the church

Key Job Responsibilities: a list of the most common and important job responsibilities (for example, interview all potential volunteers for positions)

Benefits: a list of not only paid benefits, if this is a paid position, but also the more intangible benefits such as the opportunity for growth in human relations skills. Keep in mind that the benefits need to be from the Volunteer Manager's perspective!

Qualifications: a list of non-negotiable requirements for the position (for example, is a Christian, has a bachelor's degree) and the qualifications that "would be nice" to have (for example, previous experience as a Volunteer Manager)

Supervision: Who is this person(s) responsible to, and who are they responsible for? With whom is the Volunteer Manager expected to effectively interact?

Want to see several sample job descriptions for a Volunteer Manager? See pages 109-112 for two that are currently being used in churches.

Be strategic in selecting a person to lead the volunteer ministry. This individual will play a key role in energizing the volunteers and communicating the vision of the program. A strong leader may not keep a floundering program afloat, but a poor leader will certainly sink it.

> "A strong leader may not keep a floundering program afloat, but a poor leader will certainly sink it.

Create the job description before selecting someone to fill the role. It's tempting, if you have someone in mind for the job, to design a job description that reflects the skills and experience of that person instead of the position.

Also, take care that the position as described will be respected and understood by your congregation and staff. Here's a story where that didn't happen. Don't let it become your story.

In one church, the Volunteer Ministry Manager was recruited (as an unpaid position), given a desk and enough money to create a database, and encouraged to go "do good things." The manager, a member of the church, was nominally introduced to the congregation, but it was never made clear what the vision of the ministry was, nor did the congregation truly understand what this person could and would be doing in the position.

Within a short time, the manager was highly frustrated. Her position had turned into a glorified telephone recruiter for other programs within the church. She was spending her days recruiting individuals to cook for funerals, staff the nursery, and stock the food pantry. This was *not* her vision or what she'd expected!

After a long year, she finally resigned and her resignation went virtually unnoticed. No one has stepped forward to assume the position since.

If this church *does* find another person for the position, it will have to undo the bad feelings and misunderstandings around the volunteer ministry.

What Are You Looking for in a Volunteer Manager?

Once the position is clearly and explicitly defined, think about who can best do the job. The first person to consider is a champion of the volunteer ministry. Since you're reading this book, this might be you!

Look to see who's served on the task force from the beginning. See who's focused solely on the volunteer ministry. The role will be demanding, so if the person is also singing in the choir, helping in VBS, and organizing the annual rummage sale, you're looking at someone who's too busy.

Here are some general characteristics that are good to see in your Volunteer Manager.

The Volunteer Manager is typically . . .

- Able to see potential in anyone and everyone,

- Able to perceive gifts, abilities, skills, and passions,

- A good listener,

- Assertive without being aggressive,

- A good delegator,

- Approachable,

- Comfortable interviewing people,

- A skilled manager,

- Capable of maintaining a computer database (or willing to learn how!),

- Someone who knows the congregation, and

- Someone whose enthusiasm and positive regard will *energize* the ministry!

Notice that last characteristic: enthusiasm that will energize the ministry. That's not an afterthought; it's an essential to keep the ministry on track.

Our friend and colleague, Marlene Wilson, describes herself as an "informed optimist." That means she understands that leaders and volunteers can be petty, caustic, and negative. She knows that sometimes people operate out of less-than-ideal motives. But so what? It's still her job when she's managing volunteers to draw out the best in people. To provide encouragement and vision. To keep everyone on the same page.

We think that's a good place for a Volunteer Manager to spend time: informed optimism. But not everyone is wired that way.

Being a solid manager is great—but not enough.

Being a good salesperson is great—but not enough.

You need someone who's engaging and a leader. And someone who is determined to be an informed optimist. It's that blend of positive realism that will energize your ministry from top to bottom, stem to stern.

> "It's that blend of positive realism that will energize your ministry from top to bottom, stem to stern."

So when you find the right person, how do you bring him or her on board? As a paid staff member or an unpaid volunteer staff member?

Should You Pay a Volunteer Manager—or Not?

The short answer is: It depends.

Does your congregation have the resources to pay someone to fill this role? If so, you'll have more access to that person. Your Volunteer Manager won't be fitting in the tasks and responsibilities around a money-making job.

But there's no guarantee that just because you pay someone, that will make the person perform better or that the person will be more reliable or stay in the role longer.

Still—we live in a society that tends to believe we get what we pay for. That is, if it's a paid position, the manager will be perceived as having more power and "pull" than if it's an unpaid position.

So what's the right answer? Again: It depends.

If you, as a church, feel that having a well-organized volunteer ministry is of sufficient value to invest time, energy, space, and prayer into the effort—it's not a stretch to think it's valuable enough to be worth some money, too.

Here are some relevant questions to ask—and answer—as you consider whether to create a paid staff position:

- What role in achieving your vision will the volunteer ministry have? How important will it be, given that role, to have someone in that position seen as an equal to other professionals and leaders of ministries?

- Do you have the resources to fund the position? If not, can you raise funds for that position? Are you *willing* to raise the funds?

- Do you have individuals with the skills and experience necessary to carry out the position? Will one of them be willing to accept the role as an unpaid staff member?

Some *irrelevant* questions to *not* ask are:

- Will the person be more committed if we do/don't pay him or her?

- Will the person stay with the position longer if we pay him or her?

- Can we still expect a high level of performance from this person if he or she fills the position as an unpaid volunteer staff member?

You don't ask those questions for several reasons:

"You insult the integrity of volunteers to imply they can be bought."

1. *Money doesn't buy commitment; it buys availability.* Paid staff aren't more committed than unpaid volunteers, but they're probably more available. You insult the integrity of volunteers to imply they can be bought. The best ones can't.

2. *Nobody can guarantee longevity.* If you pay a Volunteer Manager, she may move. If you pay her, she may quit. Ditto if you don't pay her.

The simple fact is that paychecks don't guarantee longevity—unless someone needs a paycheck and is stepping into the role until a full-time job can be found. In that case alone longevity is likely to be enhanced . . . but not necessarily.

3. *It's a foundational principle that we don't lower standards for volunteers.* If you'd expect a paid staffer to hit a level of excellence, expect an unpaid staff member to hit the same mark.

A colleague discovered that her pastor was growing ever more uncomfortable with her because she was serving in a full-time, unpaid position as a church Volunteer Manager. He was wondering if he could truly hold her accountable without having a paycheck as leverage. That situation is less about paychecks than the pastor's belief that only money can be a motivator and only paid ministry truly counts.

Your church can pay someone—or not. It's up to you. There are pluses and minuses on both sides of the equation, depending on what resources your church has available.

Some churches begin the Volunteer Ministry Manager role as an unpaid position, and eventually they come to value it so highly that it becomes a paid role. Other churches successfully maintain the position as an unpaid staff position.

But either way—it's a staff position. It must have the power and prestige that comes with a true staff position so the person serving as Volunteer Manager can function effectively.

> "But either way—it's a staff position."

Make the "paid/unpaid" decision through prayer and discussion, and share with your congregation how that decision was made, and why. And remember: It doesn't pay to cut corners. If you're trying to cut corners by not paying someone, where else are you cutting corners? Will you provide the funds, support, and involvement the volunteer ministry needs to be viable?

Two Ways to Support Your Volunteer Manager

First, ensure that the Volunteer Manager is directly responsible to the senior pastor or an associate pastor.

Whether the person responsible for leading your volunteer ministry is an unpaid volunteer or a paid staff member, the Director of Volunteer Ministries should be considered *at the same level as any other ministry director in your church.*

In other words, the Volunteer Ministry Director is just as important as your Music and Worship Director, your Youth Director, or your Director of Christian Education. Your

Volunteer Director needs to be on the same routing slips as other leaders, and sit in the same staff planning sessions.

The volunteer ministry exists to support every other area of ministry by finding volunteers to fill key positions. Volunteer ministry directors need to know what's going on, which ministry areas are expanding or shrinking, and what upcoming needs might be.

A second way to ensure support and nurture for your Volunteer Manager is to establish an advisory team or board. This team will provide continuous feedback and input to the ministry. As already mentioned, it can be comprised of . . .

- Representatives from the original task force,

- Program or ministry leaders from within the church,

- Other church staff members, and

- Active volunteers in the church.

Just like your original task force, the advisory team will be chartered and given job descriptions. Approach chartering an advisory team the same way you approached chartering a task force.

This team can meet periodically to give input, assess the volunteer ministry, and continue to uplift the ministry in prayer. In addition, this team can serve as ambassadors for the volunteer ministry throughout the church and into the community.

A well-chosen task force is worth its weight in gold. Work with your Volunteer Manager to create one. The right blend of people will energize your energizer, and keep him or her mindful of all the good that's being accomplished through the volunteer ministry.

In ministry, like life, little happens without energy. But energy isn't a bottomless well; without help your reserve of enthusiasm and energy will eventually be used up.

That's why you need for your ministry to be energized by more than you. You can do—and *are* doing—tremendous things. But you can't do *everything,* so you need to plug your-self and the volunteer ministry into the life-giving energy of . . .

People—both the church leadership and church membership

Vision—one that inspires, defines the program, and attracts volunteers

Mission—that provides clear purpose

Prayer—personal and corporate time with God that refreshes your heart and renews your perspective, humor, and persever-ance

The energy sizzling from these sources will empower your goals, invigorate your task force, and fortify your spirit as you continue to charge full speed ahead toward the future God has in mind for your church and your ministry.

Ready to keep going? Next you'll take practical steps to turn your vision and mission into reality!

Meeting with Leaders to Create a Volunteer Ministry

Leadership Meeting Agenda
(est. duration of meeting: 2.5 hours)

Purpose of the Meeting
To provide an overview of what a volunteer ministry is, and what it does.

To hear and understand the leadership's vision for the volunteer ministry.

To identify any barriers or concerns the leadership might perceive exist.

Desired Outcomes of the Meeting
The leadership understands the big picture of volunteer ministry.

The leaders understand their roles and what is expected of them.

Any barriers and concerns are shared.

Meeting Topic	Desired Outcome	Time
Meeting Opening: Pray, read Scripture, and review the agenda	Everyone understands why we're here	10 min.
Overview of volunteer ministry	Everyone understands the concept of volunteer ministry	15 min.
Leaders share their vision for the volunteer ministry for our church	Everyone understands the various visions from all perspectives	15 min.
Leaders discuss their roles in relation to the volunteer ministry	Agreement on each leader's roles	30 min.

Leaders identify and discuss any barriers and concerns they have regarding implementing the volunteer ministry	Barriers and concerns are listed and actions defined to address them, if possible	45 min.
Meeting closure: Next steps for the volunteer ministry, end with prayer	Everyone understands the next steps for the volunteer ministry	15 min.

Facilitator Outline for the Leadership Meeting

1. Meeting Opening
Your **purpose** is to . . .

- Focus on God's intent for the volunteer ministry.

- See that people understand the purpose and desired outcomes of the meeting.

The desired **outcomes** are:

- Everyone will seek God's will on proceeding with the volunteer ministry.

- Everyone will understand the purpose and desired outcomes of the meeting.

Open this meeting with prayer asking for God's guidance. Read Romans 12:3-8 aloud, then briefly explain how a volunteer ministry will help this process happen. Read through the desired outcomes of the meeting, and then read through the agenda topics, giving an outline of how the meeting will proceed.

2. Overview of Volunteer Ministry
Your **purpose** is to . . .

- Paint a picture of an effective church volunteer ministry.

- Identify essential components of an effective volunteer ministry.

The desired **outcomes** are . . .

- Leaders will understand how an effective volunteer ministry looks.

- Leaders will understand what it takes to create an effective volunteer ministry.

Present a model of an effective volunteer ministry. List the components that are essential (for example, interview each volunteer for placement based on gifts unique to that individual). As you go through the presentation, discuss with the leaders what is already in place and what is necessary to implement in your church.

3. Leaders Share Their Vision for the Church Volunteer Ministry

Your **purpose** is to . . .

- Give leaders the chance to explore what a volunteer ministry would be like for our church.

The desired **outcomes** are . . .

- Leaders will "catch" the vision of the volunteer ministry.

- Leaders begin to "buy in" to the work ahead.

4. Leaders Discuss Their Roles in Relation to the Volunteer Ministry

Your **purpose** is to . . .

- Help leaders understand what activities they'll be responsible for in relation to the volunteer ministry.

The desired **outcome** is . . .

- Leaders will agree on the roles they'll have in relation to the volunteer ministry.

Discuss what reporting and decision-making will be needed within the volunteer ministry. Get agreement about who will be responsible for which actions. Discuss the lines of communication needed among all the ministries and how communication will happen. Discuss expectations the leaders have of each other and the person who will be leading the volunteer ministry.

5. Leaders Will Identify and Discuss Barriers and Concerns

Your **purpose** is to . . .

- Help leaders discuss the barriers they think might impede the progress of the volunteer ministry.

- Help leaders share concerns they have about the volunteer ministry.

The desired **outcomes** are . . .

- Leaders will openly discuss barriers and concerns.

- Leaders will identify actions that will address the identified barriers and concerns.

Create a list of barriers and concerns first. On a flip chart, draw a vertical line down the middle of the page. Label the left-hand column "Barriers" and the right-hand column "Actions." Record the barriers in the left-hand column first. Then go back and ask what actions could be taken to eliminate or minimize the barriers. Assign a name and a date to the actions, if possible.

Create a list of concerns in the same way. If there are any actions that can be taken, list those with a name and a date. Some concerns may just be statements of concern, and no action can be taken.

These two lists will be helpful six months into the implementation to revisit and evaluate. Did the barriers happen? Were the concerns eliminated?

6. Meeting Closure

Your **purpose** is to . . .

- Determine the next steps to take to implement the volunteer ministry.

The desired **outcomes** are . . .

- You'll meet the desired outcomes of the meeting.

- You'll know the next steps to take to establish the volunteer ministry.

Get agreement on the next steps you can take regarding the volunteer ministry, and make them as specific as possible. Close in prayer, thanking God for working through the church leadership and for all the blessings that will flow to the congregation through the volunteer ministry.

Sample Completed Charter Document

Task Force Name: The Volunteer Ministry Task Force

Task Force Mission (Purpose):
Our mission is to explore the scope and possibilities that God intends for an organized volunteer ministry for our church.

Task Force Vision (Desired Outcomes):
When our work is done, we will clearly understand what God calls us to build in the volunteer ministry, and we will have laid the foundation for that ministry.

Task Force Sponsor:
The Church Board

The Sponsor's Role:
Two board members will sit on the task force.

Task Force Authority:
This task force can pray and discern what God intends for the volunteer ministry. This task force can engage the

congregation in what their needs are in a volunteer ministry. This task force can recommend to the board the elements necessary for a viable volunteer ministry including staff, support, space, and financial resources.

This task force cannot—without approval—spend more than $500 on research or materials.

Task Force Member Roles and Responsibilities (What tasks will be accomplished, and by whom—that is, who will call the meetings, who will facilitate the meetings):

- Maria will create and send out the agendas and facilitate the meetings.

- Tom will arrange for the meeting rooms and equipment needed.

- Jose will remind members of refreshment sign-ups.

- Ruth will type meeting notes and distribute via e-mail.

- Devotions will be shared, and members will sign up for meetings.

- Victor will write articles for the newsletter and announcements.

Task Force Time Frame:

This task force will have completed its work when the foundation for the volunteer ministry is complete and others are designated to manage the ministry. This task force may be available for a period to offer support to those who are designated.

Task Force Decision-Making (How will we make decisions?):

We'll make decisions by consensus with a fallback of a vote with a simple majority. (We define consensus as a decision that everyone can "live with" and actively support.)

Task Force Interactions (What are our ground rules?):

- We'll always do full devotions at the beginning of our meetings.

- We'll always end our meetings with prayer.

- We'll speak one at a time and listen carefully to each other.

- We'll check out assumptions before we leap to conclusions.

- We'll affirm each other for the work we are doing together.

- We'll start our meetings on time and end on time.

Task Force Interface with Others (How will this task force communicate with others?):

We'll list who we need to communicate with at the end of each meeting to ensure we are communicating the right amount of information to the right people in the right way.

Task Force Progress (How will we measure progress on the task force?):

- We'll set specific goals and measure progress on those goals at each meeting.

- We'll assess involvement of other stakeholders.

Task Force Feedback (How will we get feedback on what we are doing?):

- We'll ask for feedback when we are interacting with other groups and individuals in the church.

- We'll acknowledge the support we get from others through prayer and assistance.

Task Force Celebration (How will we celebrate progress on the task force?):

- We'll acknowledge our own achievements on our goals.

- We'll celebrate as we move forward toward our vision.

- We'll celebrate our work together when we sunset.

Title: Task Force Member Job Description

Position Summary: The Volunteer Ministry Task Force exists to explore the scope and possibilities that God intends for an organized volunteer ministry for [name of church]. Members of the task force will be committed to prayer and discernment to this end. Members will work together to assess needs of the congregation and opportunities for an organized volunteer ministry.

The task force will also assist in implementing programming to meet those needs through the creation of a volunteer ministry.

The Strategic Fit: We're called to provide nurture and care to each other as Christians. We're also called to be good stewards of the resources given to us by God. An effective and efficient volunteer ministry will help our church do and be both. Our church's vision is [fill in].

Key Job Responsibilities:

- To pray unceasingly for the volunteer ministry.

- To attend meetings to determine the scope of the volunteer ministry.

- To do work outside of meetings when requested to assess the congregation's needs.

- To assume tasks that will establish the volunteer

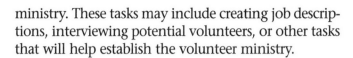

ministry. These tasks may include creating job descriptions, interviewing potential volunteers, or other tasks that will help establish the volunteer ministry.

- To follow through with people and activities to achieve the goals of the task force.

- To communicate the work of the task force with others openly and honestly.

Benefits: Being a member on the task force will provide . . .

- The opportunity to interact with other believers in the congregation.

- The chance to grow spiritually through discipline of focused prayer, reading of Scripture, and devotions.

- An opportunity to impact this ministry from the beginning.

- The opportunity to be a significant contributor to the church's vision.

Qualifications:

- It would be helpful if the task force member had some experience with this congregation.

- It will be important that the task force member has the ability and willingness to commit and follow through.

- It would be helpful if the task force member has been a volunteer within the church before.

Supervision: The task force member is responsible to the task force chair and/or the sponsor of the task force. The task force member is also responsible to honor the ground rules of the task force.

Signature of Task Force Member_____

Date _____

(Note: You can have individual members sign a charter, or do it as a group.)

Dialogue about Change Agenda

Purpose

- To explore the impact of creating a new volunteer program in our church.

Desired Outcomes

- Everyone will understand the concept of volunteer ministry you're proposing to implement.

- You will create a list of benefits of implementing the program.

- You will create a list of reasons why we need to change what we're doing now.

- You will create a list of changes/losses that people might experience.

Before the Meeting

Prior to the meeting, write the following on a flip chart page:

- Name

- How long you've attended this church

- What volunteer jobs you've held at this church

- A pleasant surprise you once received while serving in a volunteer role

Have nametags and pens to fill them out available, and ask each person to fill out and wear a nametag as he or she enters the room. Don't assume everyone knows the name of each person at the meeting. If nothing else, nametags might save you from making an embarrassing mistake!

Prepare refreshments. Use refreshments that are easy to eat while walking around talking with other people.

Introduction (15 minutes)

Begin by thanking everyone for coming.

Then ask people to introduce themselves by sharing the information on the flip chart sheet. Go first so people know how much detail you're expecting from each participant.

After each person has been introduced, offer a brief prayer in which you thank God for the volunteer contributions of the people in the room. Ask for guidance as together you all consider the future and how to best serve both God and the congregation.

Volunteer Program Overview (25 minutes)

Give a brief overview about volunteer ministry. Define it and share some context of how it plays a role in God's church. Volume 1 of this series can provide you with some thoughts to share. Be sure you include the three theologies identified in volume 1, and explain how implementing them more fully is part of your church's faithfulness in discipleship.

Ask participants to share their responses to this question:

How could our church benefit from having a better-organized volunteer program?

Record their answers on a flip chart. Be careful to accurately represent what people say. If you're unsure about something, ask.

After collecting a page or two of comments, or when the flow of comments seems to be slowing considerably, tape the comments page or pages to the wall where participants can see them.

Dialogue Prompting (30 minutes)

Indicate the suggestions and ask: **Why can't we stay here? Why can't we just keep things the way they are indefinitely?**

Again, record participants' observations. Tape the flip chart paper on the wall where participants can see them.

Say: **There's pain in making changes, but there can also be pain in staying where we are. There are consequences either way. What are the consequences of our staying where we are? We've summarized some of them on this sheet I just hung up.**

Ask for a volunteer to read through the list, framing the comments in the form of consequences. For instance, "We don't have enough nursery staff" might translate to "We won't have enough nursery workers to care for the babies of visitors."

Jot down the consequences—both positive and negative—identified by participants on a separate sheet of flip chart paper.

When you've finished, hang this consequence sheet next to the benefit sheet you created earlier.

Say: **It looks like our church could benefit from making changes in how we handle volunteer recruitment and service. Those changes will certainly stretch us, and they may be painful in some ways. But the pain we feel will be growing pains, and in time we'll find ourselves better able to serve God and our church.**

The people in this room are instrumental in deciding how volunteers are used in our church. God has used your vision and skills to accomplish much. I know we'll continue to accomplish much. As the leaders of the volunteer leadership program consider what changes to make, and what timeline to use in making them, I hope you'll continue to be active and involved . . . and available to give counsel and direction.

Refreshments (20 minutes)
Invite people to stay for refreshments, and to continue talking. Point out that your 90-minute meeting wrapped up early so there would be time for this less formal discussion time.

Be available to listen and answer questions.

Sample Volunteer Ministry Vision and Mission Statements

Sample Vision Statements

We will be a volunteer community that:

- Attracts people

- Creates a volunteer experience that enables the discovery and sharing of spiritual gifts

- Keeps volunteers connected and interested

- Meets the people's needs of the church's identified programs

Our vision is to guarantee that every volunteer is empowered, equipped to use his or her gifts, valued, trained, utilized, and appreciated.

We will increasingly become a uniquely compassionate community reflecting Christ's presence by actively serving others, actively receiving and sharing God's Word of Law and gospel, and actively lifting up prayer as the heartbeat for our daily living and for the daily life of our church.

Sample Mission Statements

The Volunteer Ministry exists to show God's love by giving of ourselves to meet the many needs of Living Hope Baptist Church.

(Living Hope Baptist Church, Bowling Green, Kentucky)

The Volunteer Services Ministry at Southeast exists to make it easy for people to connect with God, the church, and one another through volunteer service to Christ.
(Southeast Christian Church, Louisville, Kentucky)

Helping people in need and following Christ's command that we love one another lies at the heart of our Christian faith.
(Bedford Presbyterian Church, Bedford, New York)

Creating Vision and Mission Statements

Steps for Creating a Mission Statement Worksheet

1. Whom do we serve?

   _____

   _____

   _____

2. What services do we provide?

   _____

   _____

   _____

3. What's unique about us within this church?

   _____

   _____

   _____

Now, craft a simple statement:

   What's the most important phrase from everything you wrote above? (*It goes first.*)

   Then follow this first phrase with the remaining phrases.

   _____

   _____

   _____

   _____

After you have a statement, review it again and see if you can cut out any text. You want to be as brief and clear as possible. Simplify where you can.

Agenda for Mission/Vision Meeting

(est. duration of meeting: 4 hours)

Purpose of the Meeting

To create a shared mission and shared vision for the volunteer ministry

Desired Outcome of the Meeting

To reach agreement on a shared mission and shared vision

Meeting Topic	Desired Outcome	Time
Meeting Opening: Pray, introductions, and review agenda	Everyone understands why we're here and how we'll proceed for the meeting	10 min.
Introduction to volunteer ministry	Everyone understands what a volunteer ministry is	20 min.
Create a shared vision	Agreement on, at minimum, a draft of the shared vision	90 min.
Break		10 min.
Create a shared mission	Agreement on a draft of the shared mission	90 min.
Meeting closure: Thanks to all, next steps for the volunteer ministry	Meeting closure complete	20 min.

Logistics for Vision/Mission Meeting
Setting up for the meeting:

- Select a comfortable room appropriate for the anticipated number of participants.

- If possible, set up tables in a workable U-shape.

- Place flip charts where participants can easily see them.

- If serving food, put the food where it won't be a distraction.

- Make sure there's wall space for hanging individual flip chart pages.

Supplies needed for the meeting:

- Prepared flip chart pages (See pages 106-108 for content of flip charts)

- Facilitator script

- Name tent cards with participants' names printed on them

- Markers

- Masking tape for taping flip chart pages on the wall

- At least one full pad of flip chart paper

- Extra pens and pencils

- Dot stickers to use while voting

Meeting Facilitator Information and Script
1. Meeting Opening
Your **purpose** is to . . .

- Focus on God's intent for the volunteer ministry.

- Warm up the group, as some participants may have reservations and apprehension about the four hours they'll be together.

- See that people understand the purpose and desired outcomes of the meeting.

The desired **outcomes** are:

- Participants will experience the tone for the day as informal but organized.

- Everyone will understand the purpose and desired outcomes of the meeting.

Introduce yourself and your investment in the volunteer ministry. Do this by sharing your name tent, which is already filled out.

Say: **In front of you is a name tent. On the front of the tent card write the following: your name** (center), **what your volunteer role is in the church (if you have one), and the number of years you've been in this congregation.**

Lead all participants in briefly introducing themselves using the information written on their tent cards.

Say: **We have a full agenda that has room for lots of discussion. I'll make sure we stay on task and move through the agenda. Our purpose today is to come to agreement on a mission and a vision for the volunteer ministry of our church. Our desired outcomes are agreements on our statements of mission and vision.**

Lead a brief prayer asking God for wisdom and a spirit of peace and cooperation.

2. Introduction to Volunteer Ministry
Your **purpose** is to . . .

- Give all participants an understanding of what a church volunteer ministry is.

- Identify essential components of an effective volunteer ministry.

The desired **outcomes** are . . .

- Participants will understand what's included in a church volunteer ministry.

Make notes from volume 1 regarding the definition of volunteer ministry, and what elements are part of an effective ministry. Describe some success stories. You might choose to invite a member from another church that has a successful volunteer ministry to make a brief presentation at this point.

3. Create a Shared Vision
Your **purpose** is to . . .

- come to agreement on the shared vision.

The desired **outcomes** are . . .

- Participants will build a vision

- Participants will reach a consensus agreement on a draft of the vision

Present flip chart page 1.

Say: **We want to come to an agreement about why this volunteer ministry exists. We may not come out with a polished, final statement. Let me request that we follow this ground rule: If I hear you debating over words about intent, I'll let the discussion continue. If I hear you debating semantics or language preferences, we may have to stop and defer this to a smaller group to do the word-smithing. Is this okay with you?**

Say: **Here's a definition of "vision." It's a word with many meanings, but the one that will be useful to us is "Where You're Heading."**

Present flip chart page 2, then say: **A statement of vision is important to have for a number of reasons. Consider these . . .**

Read the bulleted points aloud.

Say: **We're ready to build our vision statement. Let me create a scenario for you in order to get started. We're going to fast-forward to get to the future. We are** fast-forwarding all the way to [year], five years from now. We've stopped the tape, and here we are—it's [year].

And check this out—it seems our church is now nationally recognized for our volunteer ministry. I'm a reporter assigned to your story. I need to ask you these questions: "What did you focus on to get where you are today? What did you spend your time doing?"

Present flip chart page 3.

Say: **Let's continue with the interview as I ask these questions, too. Let's work through them as I take notes on flip chart pages.**

Record participants' description of the future as they give it to you. You will most likely fill several flip chart pages with information as participants describe the future. Make sure they continue to describe something the church does *not yet have today.*

When the discussion wanes, review the list for common themes. Circle main themes with different color markers.

Say: **We're now ready to begin drafting vision statements. For this step, you'll form into small groups** [or pairs].

Form participants into different groups or pairs. Give each grouping another piece of flip chart paper and a marker.

Say: **Here are your instructions: Based on the descriptions of [year] that you came up with, give us your best shot at a vision statement. Stay concise rather than verbose. Choose a format that works for you. It can be a page, a list, a statement, symbols, graphics, art, whatever. You have about 15 minutes.**

Give a three-, two-, and one-minute countdown.

Hang the drafts in front. Stand at the wall, and have a spokesperson from each group read their group's vision statement. With *gusto*. Twice! Listen for reactions from the larger group as the statements are read. There may be one statement that has broad appeal, so it will be a good starting place for creating a common statement from the collection.

Circle common phrases, each set in a different color, or record them on a blank flip chart page, leaving spaces between phrases.

Say: **We need to come up with a combined statement that we can all live with. Give me the phrases for this combined statement.**

Record phrases on a blank flip chart page, leaving spaces between phrases. Ask participants to complete the statement with linking words. If it's taking longer than the time allotted in the agenda, you may want to assign a couple of people to finish word-smithing the statement later.

If participants *are* able to get to one statement, as a group check it against the criteria on the Checking Our Vision flip chart page. (Present flip chart page 4.)

Also, if your church has a vision statement, put that up next to the volunteer ministry statement to ensure the volunteer ministry statement aligns with the overall church statement.

Ask: **Is our vision statement one you can live with? One you can actively support?**

4. Break
Be sure you remind participants that you'll start promptly in ten minutes. Remind participants where they can find restrooms. Have snacks available.

5. Create a Shared Mission
Your **purpose** is to . . .

- come to agreement on the shared mission.

The desired **outcomes** are . . .

- Participants will build a mission

- Participants will reach a consensus agreement on a draft of the mission

Present flip chart page 5.
Say: **Here's a definition of "mission." The dictionary**

suggests several meanings, but the one that gets at what we want is "why you exist."

Present flip chart page 6.

Read the bulleted points, then say: **When we craft a mission statement, the statement is more than words. It represents the debate and discussion we've gone through to write it. It gets pulled out and used regularly. It helps us make good decisions.**

Now I'd like you to answer three questions I'll ask you one at a time. As you give me your answers, I'll write them on a page. The first question is: Who does our volunteer ministry exist to serve?

Present flip chart page 7.

Record participants' answers on the page. When participants are running out of suggestions, or they've finished the list, ask each person to select the three items on the list that he or she feels are the most important. Give each person three dots with which to vote. Tell them to put one dot next to each of their top three choices. (Note: This approach gives participants the chance to move around.)

When voting has ended, record the number of votes next to each item. Circle those with the highest votes. Hang that flip chart on a side wall.

Present flip chart page 8.

Say: **The second question that will help us create our mission is "What products and services does the volunteer ministry provide to people it serves?"**

Record participants' answers using the same voting technique you used before. Hang this flip chart next to the first flip chart on the side wall.

Present flip chart page 9.

Say: **What makes the volunteer ministry unique?**

Again, record participants' answers. This question might

take them a little longer to answer. There's no need to vote or prioritize this list. When participants are finished, hang this flip chart next to flip chart page 8.

Say: **We're now ready to begin drafting mission statements. For this step, we'll form into smaller groups** [or into pairs] **to begin writing a statement of mission.**

Form the groups and provide them with a piece of flip chart paper and a marker.

Say: **Here are your instructions: Based on these three lists, give us your best shot at a mission statement. Please write your drafts on a piece of flip chart paper, and write large enough that the group can see it when we hang it up. If you have trouble getting started, you can start with the words, "The mission of our volunteer ministry is to . . . "** You have about 15 minutes.

Give a three-, two-, and one-minute countdown.

Hang the drafts in front. Stand at the wall, and have a spokesperson from each group read their group's mission statement. With *gusto*. Twice! Listen for reactions from the larger group as the statements are read. There may be one statement that has broad appeal, so it will be a good starting place for creating a common statement from the collection.

Ask: **What common phrases do you see that are being repeated from statement to statement?** Draw a circle around common phrases, each in a different color, or record them on a blank flip chart page, leaving spaces between phrases.

Say: **We need to come up with a combined statement that we can all live with. Could we start with one of these statements** [the one that got the most positive reaction] **and add, change, or delete to create your shared mission?**

If so, start on a clean sheet. If not, suggest to the group the following . . . **Look at the common phrases and tell me what's the most important of these? Let's begin with that. Give me the other phrases for this combined statement.**

Ask participants to complete the statement with linking words. If it looks like they'll not be able to arrive at a shared

statement within the time allotted in the agenda, suggest that a smaller team continue to word-smith the statement.

If participants *are* able to get to one statement, as a group check it against the criteria on the Checking Our Mission flip chart page. (Present flip chart page 10.)

Also, if your church has a mission statement, put that up next to the volunteer ministry statement to ensure the volunteer ministry statement aligns with the overall church statement.

Ask: **Is our mission statement one you can live with? One you can actively support?**

6. Meeting Closure

Thank everyone for coming and investing their time in the volunteer ministry. Explain the next steps you'll be taking to launch or rekindle the volunteer ministry.

Prepared Flip Charts for Mission/Vision Meeting

Flip chart page 1
Vision: Where you're headed

Flip chart page 2
Why vision?

- It embodies the tension between today and desired future.

- It provides a sense of direction.

- It's a tool that communicates where the organization wants to be.

- It provides a framework for opportunity and selection.

- It allows members to be energized about what is yet to happen.

Flip chart page 3

What's Happening Five Years from Now?

- What are clients getting from our organization?

- What do we see going on in and around here?

- What does our organization look like?

- What do our clients look like?

- Who does our organization have relationships (part-nerships) with?

- What new needs are we meeting?

- Where are we spending our time?

- Where are we spending our money?

- How would we describe what has changed most in the last five years?

Flip chart page 4

Checking Our Vision Statement
Is our statement of vision . . .

- Outcome focused, describing where we want to be in five years?

- Actionable—can we write goals and vision priorities based on it?

- Simple, yet compelling?

Flip chart page 5

Mission: Why we exist

Flip chart page 6

Why mission?

- Allows the volunteer ministry to focus on what's truly important.

- The ministry can prioritize which problems to address.

- Allows for conflict resolution.

- Prioritizes where people spend time, energy, and resources for the volunteer ministry.

- Creates synergy.

Flip chart page 7
Who does our volunteer ministry exist to serve?

Flip chart page 8
What products and services does the volunteer ministry provide to people it serves?

Flip chart page 9
What makes the volunteer ministry unique?

Flip chart page 10
Checking Our Mission Statement

- Does our statement of mission clearly describe why we exist?

- Is our statement of mission inspiring to all of us?

- Is it demonstrable? Can we see how our assets have been used toward the mission?

- As written, does our statement of mission provide us with clarity for making decisions?

- As written, will our statement of mission keep us focused on what's truly important?

Volunteer Ministry Manager Sample Job Descriptions

Sample 1

Position Description

Membership Ministries Coordinator
First Presbyterian Church of Granville, Ohio

Job Summary

The Membership Ministries Coordinator helps members and friends of the church to identify and claim their gifts, talents, and areas of interest for personal growth, and helps them to identify areas of ministry. The Membership Ministries Coordinator identifies and profiles needs of the church and its ministry, both within the congregation and outside of the church in mission areas.

Purpose of the Position

An important but often neglected spiritual ministry of the church is to call forth, name, and encourage the use of the gifts of members. These gifts have their source in God and are best expressed in some form of Christian service. The Membership Ministries Coordinator takes the lead in coordinating this ministry of gifts and assisting members and friends in linking their interests and abilities with the needs of the church and the world.

Authority

The Membership Ministries Coordinator reports to the pastor who has responsibility for membership, and is a member of the staff, attending one staff meeting per month.

Responsibilities

- Develop goals, actions, and budget at least annually.

- Develop, or supervise the development of, job descriptions for volunteer positions.

- Regularly interview and assist members and friends of the church to identify their gifts and talents, areas for personal growth, and their sense of calling.

- Maintain a current database containing this information. Assist with their integration into service.

- Maintain support systems for volunteers: placement, training, supervision, feedback, and recognition.

- Regularly profile the needs of the church, both within the congregation and outside of the church in its areas of mission. Maintain a current database containing this information.

- Assist church leaders as they recruit volunteers for their needs.

- Communicate regularly throughout the congregation to keep members and friends informed.

- Keep current on congregational events, issues, initiatives, opportunities, and challenges.

Qualifications for Position
The candidate will possess management skills, will know the congregation, will work well with a variety of people, will be present during worship on Sunday, and will be motivated by the creative possibilities within the life of the congregation.

Terms of the Position
The duties and performance within this position will be reviewed annually by the Head of Staff. The position requires 10 hours per week and is a volunteer position.

Sample 2

Position Description
Title: Coordinator of Volunteer Ministry
Department: Outreach Ministries
Reports To: Associate Pastor of Outreach Ministries

Objective

To increase and maximize the number of volunteer opportunities and match more members to those opportunities. To promote spiritual growth by the concept that each person is serving in ministry when they respond to their faith as members of Christ's church (that is, priesthood of all believers, whole body of Christ, and giftedness of each child of God).

Specific Responsibilities/Duties

- Design and implement volunteer recruitment strategies to encourage more involvement from the congregation.

- Develop, or supervise the development of, job descriptions for volunteer positions.

- Design and implement volunteer retention strategies.

- Develop and maintain appropriate systems (such as one-on-one interviews) to help match members' gifts, talents, and abilities to appropriate and meaningful ministry opportunities.

- Develop procedures to involve the members in ministry opportunities, and follow up on placements of volunteers.

- Develop and maintain up-to-date records concerning volunteer services within the congregation.

- Present information about the volunteer ministry at all New Member classes.

- Serve as a resource person to church staff and lay leaders:

—Help them work with volunteers in designing strategies for the recruitment and retention of volunteers for their respective ministries

—Help them initiate training for volunteers as needed, and

—When necessary (and subject to the approval of the Associate Pastor of Outreach Ministries), personally contact church members to recruit them as volunteers.

• Facilitate recognition and appreciation for volunteers in ongoing and meaningful ways.

• Participate as a team member of staff, including attending staff meetings and regularly attending worship services at [church].

• Be available for other assignments and projects as needed and assigned.

Qualifications:
Faith/Spiritual Life: Committed Christian, with a strong Christian faith. Maintains a Christian lifestyle and active devotional life. Actively demonstrates Christian faith through lifestyle and actions.
Abilities/Skills: Good planning and organizational skills. Good communication skills, both written and verbal. Demonstrates strong teamwork and strong interpersonal skills. Goal-oriented and resourceful. Good knowledge of self and personal and spiritual gifts.
Education/Training: B.A. in Education or related field preferred. Training or experience in volunteer ministries or recruiting volunteers preferred. Experience working with and directing people. Experience working as a volunteer. Experience working with a variety of computer programs.

This is a part-time position. Salary of $1,250/month, 25 hours weekly (average). Hours may include daytime, evening, weekend, and holiday work.